Classics

Polity's *Why It Matters* series

In these short and lively books, world-leading thinkers make the case for the importance of their subjects and aim to inspire a new generation of students.

Lynn Hunt, *History*
Tim Ingold, *Anthropology*
Neville Morley, *Classics*

Neville Morley

———

Classics

Why It Matters

polity

The right of Neville Morley to be identified as Author of this Work has been asserted in accordance with the UK Copyright, Designs and Patents Act 1988.

First published in 2018 by Polity Press

Polity Press
65 Bridge Street
Cambridge CB2 1UR, UK

Polity Press
101 Station Landing
Suite 300
Medford, MA 02155, USA

ISBN-13: 978-1-5095-1792-3
ISBN-13: 978-1-5095-1793-0 (pb)

A catalogue record for this book is available from the British Library.

Typeset in 11 on 15 Sabon by Servis Filmsetting Ltd, Stockport, Cheshire
Printed and bound in the UK by CPI Group (UK) Ltd, Croydon

The publisher has used its best endeavours to ensure that the URLs for external websites referred to in this book are correct and active at the time of going to press. However, the publisher has no responsibility for the websites and can make no guarantee that a site will remain live or that the content is or will remain appropriate.

Every effort has been made to trace all copyright holders, but if any have been inadvertently overlooked the publisher will be pleased to include any necessary credits in any subsequent reprint or edition.

For further information on Polity, visit our website: politybooks.com

Contents

1

What's Wrong with Classics

The Foundations of Knowledge

Why does classics – the study of the societies and cultures of the ancient Mediterranean world, and their literary and artistic products – matter? Five hundred years or so ago, such a question would have seemed entirely absurd: knowledge of the works of the ancient Greeks and Romans *was* knowledge as commonly understood by the educated elites of Europe, the foundation of all understanding of the natural world, human society and politics, and art. (Its relation to the spiritual world and to the truth revealed by Holy Scripture was a rather more contentious issue.) Latin was already the trans-European language of learning and law, thanks to the Church, and it remained the basis of all education, even when humanist scholars in the fifteenth and sixteenth centuries started to develop alternative schemes of education in place of the curricula offered by Church institutions. Latin thus became the indispensable medium for all scientific and intellectual communication, the language in which figures such as Newton, Leibniz and Descartes published their most important works, so that their ideas could reach an audience across the continent. Since Latin was taught at higher levels through the medium of classical Roman texts, even the least historically minded pupil imbibed a substantial dose of Roman literature and culture in the process, whether or not they remembered any of the language, and classical names and references were as familiar in the conversations and letters of the educated classes as anything from the literature and history of their own countries.

More importantly, learning classical languages was the best means to access the store of classical knowledge and wisdom. The period of dramatic intellectual and cultural activity we know as the Renaissance, beginning in fourteenth-century Italy and spreading across the rest of western Europe over the next two hundred years, was conceived as the *re*-birth of classical learning, recovering it from obscurity and religious suppression so that it could be put into practice once more in the hope of matching the cultural achievements of the Greeks and Romans. Initially through Latin authors alone, and then gradually also through their classical Greek predecessors – above all after the fall of Constantinople in 1453 and the subsequent westwards migration of Greek speakers and their texts – the full breadth of ancient learning was put at the disposal of the new Europe. Scholars laboured to improve the quality of the texts, recognizing that the process of copying and re-copying them over the centuries had introduced errors and variations. Some endeavoured to recover forgotten (or deliberately suppressed) works from obscure libraries or by reading between the lines (literally) of manuscripts known as palimpsests, where pages of writers like Tacitus or Ovid had been reused for a later Christian work but the original could still be deciphered. Others worked to make this knowledge more widely available, translating Greek texts into Latin and Latin ones into vernacular languages, such as Thomas North's English translation of the *Parallel Lives* of Plutarch, which provided Shakespeare with several plots and a great many references, or Thomas Hobbes' version of Thucydides, which influences political theory to this day.

Classical wisdom was regarded as the fount of all knowledge. Science began with Aristotle, followed by figures like Theophrastus and Ptolemy, with Galen for medicine; philosophy began with Plato and Aristotle, and was continued by Cicero and Seneca; historiography had been invented by Herodotus and Thucydides, while Livy, Sallust and Tacitus offered further guidance on how one should write the history of a nation or a ruler, as well as providing ideas for political theorists like Machiavelli and Hobbes and rhetorical models for aspiring young politicians; the campaigns of Alexander and Caesar, and ancient handbooks of strategy and tactics, informed the latest military science; Plutarch, both because of his *Lives* of exemplary Greeks and Romans and because of his vast output of improving maxims, was virtually a complete education in how one ought to comport oneself in the world. Artists, meanwhile, looked to the achievements of the ancients in poetry, drama, sculpture and architecture, and to the ideas developed by figures like Aristotle on tragedy, Quintilian on rhetoric, Ovid on poetry and Vitruvius on architecture about how these works achieved their effects and what rules practitioners ought to follow. Not even the sphere of 'everyday life' was spared: agricultural handbooks, such as the one written by Varro, were adopted as sources of important advice for any estate owner, despite the fact that, to our eyes, they were manifestly dealing with an entirely different world.

The importance of the works of the Greeks and Romans, as a source of knowledge, understanding, and practical and theoretical wisdom, was undisputed – though the scope for debate about *which* classical authority one should follow, when inevitably one came across a difference of opinion or of practice, was enormous. There were questions to be asked about the relation of such learning to the biblical and scriptural tradition, which continued well into the nineteenth century: did one seek to reconcile the different perspectives that classical and scriptural sources offered on certain topics, such as the nature of the universe or the role of divinity (singular or plural) or apparently divergent historical narratives, or decide the conflict in favour of one or the other, or simply evade the issue? A still more pressing problem, at least for artists and scientists, was how far it might be possible for people of the post-classical age to match or even surpass their ancient predecessors in different fields. The greatness of the classical achievement was not in any question, but was it complete and perfect, so that the moderns could only imitate, choose between classical authorities or provide at best minor footnotes on already-established knowledge?

Ancients and Moderns

Even in the mid-seventeenth century, it was clear to many that the 'ancient' position, requiring total submission to classical authority, was untenable. In the fields of science, mathematics and technology, modern research and investigative techniques not only went far beyond the achievements of the ancients but in important respects (the structure of the solar system, for example) contradicted their claims, as well as those of biblical authority. Even if one adopted the view put forward by William Temple in his 1690 attack on the progressivists of the Royal Society, 'On Ancient and Modern Learning', that the moderns could see further because they were standing on the shoulders of giants, this was a clear admission that ancient authority was not in itself *sufficient* or complete. Increasingly, therefore, classical learning became less central as modern knowledge and understanding accumulated. The usefulness of Latin in this context was that it allowed communication with fellow scientists across linguistic boundaries, rather than because it gave access to the treasury of ancient thought – and so it was seen as a basic skill associated with one's schooldays, rather than necessarily a matter of lifelong interest. Belief in the eternal validity of ancient aesthetic principles persisted rather longer – and indeed there were periodic reassertions of the centrality of the classical as a model for artists, for example in the late eighteenth century as the result of J. J. Winckelmann's magisterial studies of classical sculpture, presenting works like the 'Apollo Belvedere' (Figure 1) as the epitome of 'noble simplicity and quiet grandeur'. However, adherence to classical norms was increasingly an artistic choice,

Figure 1: The 'Apollo Belvedere': Roman copy (second century CE) of lost Greek bronze (fourth century BCE). Classical perfection? (Getty Images)

one aesthetic possibility among many, rather than the sole acceptable form. One might, as the seventeenth-century French playwright Jean Racine did, choose not only to write tragedies based on classical plots, but also to adhere firmly to the principles of the Aristotelian theory of tragedy, even though many classical tragedies departed from that norm – but plenty of his contemporaries explored different approaches to the theatre. John Milton's *Paradise Lost* is manifestly an attempt to rival ancient epic, and to explore what it means to write an epic in a Christian context, as much as it is influenced by or imitating ancient models.

Moreover, there was a growing awareness of the differences between the present and the classical past in material and social terms, which raised questions about the validity and usefulness of classical knowledge. Quite simply, the world was changing, to the point where this became impossible to ignore: in the development of the European economy and the adoption of new productive technology, for example, leading to an increase in material prosperity and power over nature that went far beyond anything the ancients could manage. The consequences of these changes could still be interpreted in classical terms – some denounced them as 'luxury', and prophesied social and moral disaster as a result, just as Sallust had shown Rome becoming corrupted by its increasing wealth – but it was difficult to argue persuasively that the ancient world had actually experienced such an economic and technological revolution. New forms of knowledge – political economy and other embryonic social sciences – offered alternative explanations of modern developments. These promised the moderns not only that they could understand their own world, but also that they could turn these intellectual tools back towards the past, and understand the world of the Greeks and Romans better than they did themselves. From this perspective, classical antiquity comes to appear underdeveloped, even primitive; far from being the pinnacle of all civilization which we moderns can only try to imitate, it is seen instead as a point of origin, which modern Europe has now surpassed and from which it will continue to diverge.

This historical development was not always seen positively: for every celebration of the new power and dynamism of modernity, science and reason, we can find a lament for the loss of wholeness, authenticity, spirit and beauty as a result of our distance from antiquity. 'Where now, as our wise men tell us, a ball of fire revolves soullessly, then Helios drove his golden chariot in silent majesty,' sighed the German poet Friedrich Schiller in his 'The Gods of Greece' of 1788.[1] Admiration for Greek culture, which reached new heights in the eighteenth and nineteenth centuries, provoked the question of why modern artists were incapable of matching it, despite all the advantages of their society. Is Achilles – that is, the whole epic tradition of heroism and myth – possible with power and lead, and with the printing press, wondered Karl Marx. Why should we feel such nostalgia for the cultural products of a more 'primitive' age?[2] The theme of a demythologized, disenchanted modernity persists today, as we see in the insistence of the poet Kate Tempest that modern life is *not* completely rubbish:

> our colours *are* muted and greyed
> but our battles are staged all the same
> and we are still mythical . . .
> But the plight of a people who have forgotten their
>   myths
> and imagine that somehow now is all that there is
> is a sorry plight,
> all isolation and worry . . . .[3]

This slow process of differentiation between ancient and modern, and the growing belief in progress (or at least change) and superiority (or at least difference), did not mean that knowledge of the classical ceased entirely to be relevant. In some respects, such knowledge was understood to be more important, as a means of understanding the roots of modern European civilization and its particular nature and dynamics. The search for European origins, coupled with a growing sense that the familiar sources needed to be evaluated, criticized and tested against other evidence, gave impetus to ever more sophisticated research into the classical past, especially its material rather than just its textual remains. The rediscovery of the monuments of classical Greece in the eighteenth century, and the continuing tradition of the Grand Tours made by the children of the northern European elites to the Mediterranean, taking in many classical sites, reinforced the notion of a special connection between classical Greece and Rome and the civilization of modern western Europe – at the same time establishing a new myth of origin, presenting the modern Europeans as the true and direct heirs of that classical civilization. Classical knowledge was still valued in at least some spheres of intellectual activity, even if not in science: Plato and Aristotle retained their pride of place in philosophy well into the twentieth century, as did Thucydides in historiography, while classical myth in different forms continued to supply artists and writers with powerful, malleable material. The architecture of the ancient world remained an important model – not least for imperial powers like France and Britain, as a template for how world domination should be expressed and magnified in stone.

But art in the modern world continued to demand novelty, the reworking of plastic material rather than slavish imitation of ancient models, and the development of new forms of representation suitable for the new forms of society. Classical culture had little to offer the quintessentially modern creations of the novel and the symphony. Classical forms were associated ever more closely with safe, conservative, bourgeois tastes; if modernism engaged with classical antiquity at all, it took the raw stuff of myth and emphasized its unclassical rawness, whether Pablo Picasso's Minotaurs (1935), Stravinsky's *Oedipus rex* (1927) or James Joyce's Dublin reworking of the *Odyssey* in *Ulysses* (1922), where barmaids and prostitutes take the place of Sirens and Circe, and the received language of classical poetry and the poetry of everyday speech are bundled promiscuously together:

Ah! Ow! Don't be talking! I was blue mouldy for the want of that pint. Declare to God I could hear it hit the pit of my stomach with a click.

And lo, as they quaffed their cup of joy, a godlike messenger came swiftly in, radiant as the eye

12

of heaven, a comely youth and behind him there passed an elder of noble gait and countenance, bearing the sacred scrolls of law and with him his lady a dame of peerless lineage, fairest of her race.[4]

Joyce's novel draws on the inherited power of classical stories, but classical grandeur and nobility are introduced only to be mocked, rejecting any idea of the innate superiority of the past.

The Invention of Classics

Classics as an academic discipline, as a distinct branch of knowledge with its own rules and customary practices, emerges in the second half of the eighteenth century out of the collapse of the authority of the classical. Of course the subject could trace its lineage, and many of its scholarly habits and pedagogical techniques – the set of skills in the analysis of texts and languages often labelled 'philology' – back to the Renaissance humanists and beyond. But whereas for the scholars of the early modern period classical knowledge and languages were like water to fish, the environment within which they lived and beyond which existence was simply inconceivable, intellectual life had now developed legs and embarked on the exploration of the land. Hardly anyone – and certainly few of those doing serious scientific research or engaging with the problems of the present – now wrote in Latin as anything other than a display of scholarly virtuosity; proficiency in classical languages was now developed as a skill that enabled the study of the texts of the past, rather than any contemporary purpose. Education at school and university level increasingly made space for other, more obviously useful, subjects.

Moreover, centuries of scholarly effort to translate the works of the Greeks and Romans into more accessible forms meant that a speaker of one of the major European languages could access the landmarks of classical culture and learning without requiring any knowledge of their original language. Other scholars had laboured to produce more convenient (and, arguably, more accurate) accounts of Greek and Roman history and thought, consolidating and synthesizing the different works of ancient historians to produce a more critical, consistent narrative. Artists and architects drew inspiration from viewing classical artworks and buildings themselves, or from studying copies and imitations and illustrations; creative writers whose grasp of the ancient languages was, for whatever reason, limited or non-existent could still encounter classical culture in more accessible forms, through adaptations of Greek tragedy, retellings of myth or translations and paraphrases. As John Keats remarked of his encounter with George Chapman's 1616 version of Homer:

> Oft of one wide expanse had I been told
> That deep-browed Homer ruled as his demesne;
> Yet did I never breathe its pure serene
> Till I heard Chapman speak out loud and bold.
> . . .[5]

It's important to stress that what Keats is offering here is not a contrast between an English version of Homer and the 'real' Greek one, but a comparison of different approaches to rendering Homer's poems in English, preferring Chapman's 'vigorous' and rather free version to the more elegant (and much more classically erudite and accurate) later translations produced by Alexander Pope or John Dryden. Keats was mocked by contemporaries for his lack of a proper classical education – for some, even relying on Pope or Dryden was a sign of intellectual inferiority – but this proved no impediment to his powerful imaginative engagement with the presence of the classical past in the present.

The cultural products of classical antiquity continued to offer inspiration to the moderns in many different fields of intellectual activity, even as they lost ground in others; however, one might question whether this ongoing influence necessitated the establishment of an academic discipline to service it. It was not just that one might now access the finest products of ancient culture without any serious knowledge of Latin or Greek; it was also the possibility that scholarly research into the period might be better served by disciplines other than philology. The history of Greece and Rome, for example, could be entrusted to historians, who drew on a wider range of evidence than just the literary monuments of the period, not least the material evidence that was being gathered in increasing quantities, and who could also develop useful comparisons with other ancient civilizations. The study of Roman law was already largely in the hands of legal scholars rather than Latin experts – so why not also the study of philosophy, of politics, of society, and so forth? If classics, in the sense of the legacy of Greek and Roman culture, matters and continues to matter, this is not automatically true of classics in the sense of the academic discipline. In successive upheavals over the nineteenth and twentieth centuries, with the foundation of new universities and multiple reforms to the curricula at all levels of education, classics was constantly threatened with dissolution or partition between other academic disciplines, with reduction to, at best, a rump of language teaching while the interpretation of antiquity was pursued, if at all, by those who identified themselves as historians or philosophers or art historians rather than as classicists. The reality of this threat (if it's perceived as a threat) can be seen in the fact that plenty of universities, especially outside the UK, place ancient history in the history department, classical philosophy among the philosophers and the study of material remains within archaeology, rather than ceding full responsibility for all things classical to the philologists and their associates.

The success of classics in coming through these upheavals and establishing itself as a still-prestigious subject in schools and universities in the nineteenth century, defining a distinctive role against upstart rivals like history, continues to shape the position and status of the discipline today. We can get some sense of the necessary manoeuvring in the early years of the century from an 1809 essay by the philosopher G.W.F. Hegel, 'On Classical Studies', where he reflected on the newly introduced German educational system in which Latin 'has lost the dignity so long claimed for it, the dignity of being the universal and almost the sole foundation of education. It has ceased to be considered as an end in itself.' This, Hegel argued, is entirely appropriate, given the enormous differences between ancient and modern:

> Are we not entitled to assume that the achievements of modern times, our illumination and the progress of all arts and sciences, have worn out the Greek and Roman garments of their childhood and outgrown their leading strings, so that they can now advance on their own territory without hindrance?[6]

This sense of the differences between past and present might be taken as grounds for downgrading the study of the classical altogether; the works of the ancients 'would have to be ranked with memories and superfluous learning antiquities, with things of merely historical import'. That, Hegel argued, would be far too narrow and restrictive, a betrayal of the true nature and purpose of education.

> If we agree that excellence should be our starting-point, then the foundation of higher study must be and remain Greek literature in the first place, Roman in the second. . . . For this initiation a general, perfunctory acquaintance with the ancients is not sufficient; we must take up our lodging with them so that we can breathe their air, absorb their ideas, their manners, one might even say their errors and prejudices, and become at home in this world – the fairest that ever has been.[7]

Education, for Hegel, is not merely about knowledge; it is about the development of the mind and soul. That high purpose requires a continuing engagement with the most perfect masterpieces of human creativity, those produced by the classical world, and *that* requires no mere casual acquaintance, but a deep and lasting relationship – fully physical and immersive, breathing the ancients' air, absorbing their manners and their prejudices.

Hegel's essay encapsulates several important intellectual moves that are still found in many modern attempts at defending classics as a discipline. The excellence, perfection and glory of the cultural products of the Greeks and Romans are taken for granted, and are connected to their culture as a whole and indeed to their qualities as human beings. Further, it is *only* classical culture that should concern us, as part of our European heritage, because it is simply superior to the civilizations of other regions of the world; the Chinese or Indians may have their own 'classics', but they are primitive and alien in comparison. This is not about mere knowledge, or even just identification with the past, but a complete initiation into the cult of the ancients, an attempt to enter into their world and to become as much like them as possible – again, because they are perceived as superior beings and a model for human development. Such a full immersion into the past can occur only through direct engagement with the authentic products of classical culture, based on an intimate knowledge of the original languages as the key to the ancients' thought – not filtered through a deficient and partial translation, someone else's inadequate rendition of their ideas. Classical civilization is conceived in terms of its most refined spiritual and intellectual products, happily ignoring any vulgarities or less desirable aspects of the past, and not worrying about the fact that the surviving texts represent only a small proportion of the inhabitants of classical antiquity. In brief: classics matters because Greek and Roman culture is the pinnacle of human achievement, the means to a higher plane of being and understanding – and classics as a discipline matters because only it can induct you into the chosen band of initiates.

Hegel's idealistic views were of course somewhat idiosyncratic. Other proponents of the classics, for example in British public schools, added more pragmatic arguments to the idea of the innate superiority of classical culture. There is the familiar claim that studying classical languages gives a young man (because this was above all a matter of the education of boys) a better understanding of his own language (especially as the rules of vernacular

grammar were often formulated in order to conform to Latin – though not, as is often asserted, the
prohibition of the split infinitive). Philological skills
were claimed as an ideal basis for all kinds of critical
and analytical thought – whereas English literature
is just reading, something one does for pleasure
rather than as a serious academic study, and natural
scientists merely learn by rote and perform experi-
ments like automatons. At the same time, we find
the claim that classics was the appropriate study for
a gentleman precisely because it was not utilitar-
ian, but focused on the development of the mind
and spirit. Classics becomes the epitome of aristocratic male education, an idea reinforced in Britain
by the historical accident that classical languages
remained a requirement for admission to Oxford
and Cambridge well into the twentieth century.
As well as reinforcing the subject's prestige as a
status marker, this created a continuing demand for
classics teachers in the schools of the elite, a cadre
with a vested interest in self-perpetuation; as Nigel
Molesworth, caustic observer of the British education system in the 1950s, remarked: 'anyway latin
masters would be out of a job if there was no latin
so they keep it going.'[8] Classics fed off the continuing prestige of its subject matter, and its ideological
power as a marker of the cultural superiority of the

triumphant imperialist West. A classicist was the sort of well-rounded chap one wanted to go out and rule the empire, and to take the fruits of his learning with him to enlighten the ignorant inhabitants of the world beyond Europe.

'We Classicists'

Generations of schoolboys have sat through classics lessons as a conventional part of European elite education; generations of classics teachers have offered such claims about the importance of classical studies. One dissenting voice was that of a classics professor who became increasingly dissatisfied with the whole enterprise – not least by the sceptical if not nakedly hostile response of more or less the entire German classical profession to his first book, in which he sought to demonstrate the real, living, vital relevance of classical learning to the present.

> Our culture is built upon a wholly castrated and mendacious study of antiquity. In order to see how ineffective this study is, one simply looks at the philologists: they ought to be the most highly cultivated men through their study of antiquity. Are they?[9]

What's Wrong with Classics

Well, no, not by Friedrich Nietzsche's standards; his unpublished essay 'We Classicists' ('Wir Philologen') was a ferocious denunciation of classics as an academic discipline, for its failure to grasp the true nature and meaning of antiquity – and its failure to recognize his own contribution in *The Birth of Tragedy* (1872), published and largely ignored by his colleagues a few years earlier. Contemporary classicists, Nietzsche argued, have a tendency towards the ridiculous idealization of the classical past, and consequently misunderstand the true complexity and power of the ancient world: 'They lack the real desire for the strong and powerful traits of antiquity. They become eulogists and thereby become ridiculous.' At the same time, they are failures both as educators and men:

On enquiring into the origin of the classicist I find: 1. A young man cannot have the slightest conception of what the Greeks and Romans were. 2. He does not know whether he is fitted to investigate into them. 3. And, in particular, he does not know to what extent, in view of the knowledge he may actually possess, he is fitted to be a teacher. What then enables him to decide on this path is not the knowledge of himself or his science; but (a) imitation, (b) the convenience of carrying on the kind of work which he had begun at school, (c) his intention

of earning a living. In short, ninety-nine classicists
out of a hundred *should* not be classicists at all.

Nietzsche marked his own contempt for the enterprise
first by trying to transfer to a chair in philosophy,
and then by abandoning academia altogether after
his health deteriorated. His conception of classical
studies, like his views on many other matters, was
undoubtedly eccentric, going far beyond the limits of
normal scholarship – and all the more exciting and
provocative as a result. 'Philology of the Future!' was
the derisive title of an article attacking *The Birth of
Tragedy* by the future doyen of German classicists,
Ulrich von Wilamowitz-Moellendorf. That phrase
might have given a less self-confident and less dog-
gedly conservative man pause. Did he really mean
to imply that the study of antiquity could only ever
be of the past, a dry and narrow analysis of a static
body of knowledge?

Certainly that is the impression of classicists
and their intellectual activities offered by modern
writers; unfair caricatures, perhaps, but this gives
us an impression of the standing of classics, for
all its inherited prestige, in the eyes of the more
progressive sectors of European culture. Take the
first appearance of Mr Casaubon, a middle-aged
clergyman dedicated to the compilation of a *Key*

to All Mythologies, in George Eliot's *Middlemarch* (1871–2):

> I have little leisure for such literature just now. I have been using up my eyesight on old characters lately; the fact is, I want a reader for my evenings; but I am fastidious in voices, and I cannot endure listening to an imperfect reader. It is a misfortune, in some senses: I feed too much on the inward sources; I live too much with the dead. My mind is something like the ghost of an ancient, wandering about the world and trying mentally to construct it as it used to be, in spite of ruin and confusing changes. But I find it necessary to use the utmost caution about my eyesight.[10]

At this point, the heroine Dorothea is convinced that he is the most interesting man she has ever met – a sign of her own limited education, as a mere girl. 'To reconstruct a past world, doubtless with a view to the highest purposes of truth – what a work to be in any way present at, to assist in, though only as a lamp-holder!'[11] The reader, less willing to allow that 'doubtless', silently screams at her to get out while she can, and is forced to watch how Casaubon's coldness, pedantry and selfishness grind away at her spirit for much of the novel. His grasp of the dead world of the past is shaky, and he offers nothing to the living.

The contrast between subject matter and scholar is a recurrent theme, as in W.B. Yeats' poem 'The Scholars' (1914/15), where

> Bald heads forgetful of their sins,
> Old, learned, respectable bald heads
> Edit and annotate the lines
> That young men, tossing on their beds,
> Rhymed out in love's despair
> To flatter beauty's ignorant ear.[12]

'They'll cough in the ink to the world's end;/ Wear out the carpet with their shoes'; they turn the passionate outpourings of true poets into mere scholarship, stripping out everything physical and emotional in favour of technical analysis. 'Did their Catullus walk that way?' Of course not. How can classical culture work to make its students more civilized and human when it has been processed into journal articles and language exercises?

Other poets in this period raised questions about the sentiments of the Latin poetry actually taught in schools – nothing as racy as Catullus, of course – and the uses to which they were put: 'The old Lie,' Wilfred Owen wrote in 1917: '*Dulce et decorum est pro patria mori* [It is sweet and proper to die for ones' country].'[13] The values which classical education was used to inculcate, patriotism and public duty, led not to civilization and peace but to the nightmare of the trenches. Thirty years later, in Thomas Mann's novel *Doktor Faustus* (1947), the elderly classics teacher Serenus Zeitblom watches impotently as Germany falls into flames, just as he had helplessly watched the decline and madness of his friend, the inspired composer Adrian Leverkühn. Not only had classical humanism once again failed to prevent the horrors of the twentieth century, it formed part of their roots, as shown in the conversations of Zeitblom, Leverkühn and their clever friends in their student days. Just like Mussolini's fascists, with their re-creations of imperial Rome, Nazism drew on the symbolic power of classical forms, in sculpture and architecture, and on the classical tradition of idealizing purity, beauty and strength.

The perverse fruit of an idealized antiquity was scarcely confined to Italy and Germany, or to the mid-twentieth century. In the European empires of the nineteenth century, it justified the subjugation, exploitation and murder of millions, on the grounds of the natural superiority of the conquerors and their civilization, their re-creation of the glories of the Roman Empire on a global scale. In the United States, ancient ideas of the freedom and equality of all citizens, incorporated into rousing declarations about the right to life, liberty and the pursuit of happiness, sat happily alongside ancient justifications of the reduction of inferior human types to the status of exploitable property – Aristotle's idea of 'natural slavery'. Even now, when slavery has been abolished, claims about the innate superiority of white civilization, grounded in the achievements of classical antiquity, persist as an explanation and excuse for inequality and racial injustice. In the eyes of the Caribbean poet Derek Walcott, exploring the complex meanings of Homer in a non-European, post-colonial context, the shadows of slavery and its legacy are inseparable from the celebration of the classical legacy:

> small squares with Athenian principles and pillars
> maintained by convicts and emigrants who had
>   fled
> persecution and gave themselves *fasces* with laws
> to persecute slaves. A wedding-cake Republic.
> Its domes, museums, its ornate institutions,
> its pillared façade that looked down on the black
> shadows that they cast as an enraging nuisance
> which, if it were left to its Solons, with enough
>   luck
> would vanish from its cities, just as the Indians
> had vanished from its hills. . . .[14]

Rather than contrasting the glorious classicized image of the United States with the violence of its foundation, Walcott sees them as inextricably linked, the black shadows cast by the gleaming white wedding-cake architecture – perpetually enraging to those who seek to deny America's shameful past.

A Class Act

It is no coincidence that the archetypal English public school teacher, in James Hilton's *Goodbye, Mr Chips* (1934), was a classicist, even if not a very good one.

> He was not, despite his long years of assiduous teaching, a very profound classical scholar; indeed, he thought of Latin and Greek far more as dead languages from which English gentlemen ought to know a few quotations than as living tongues that had ever been spoken by living people. He liked those short leading articles in the *Times* that introduced a few tags that he recognized. To be among the dwindling number of people who understood such things was to him a kind of secret and valued freemasonry; it represented, he felt, one of the chief benefits to be derived from a classical education.[15]

Mr Chipping gives the game away: the continued role of Latin (and to a lesser extent Greek) in the British system of private education and elite universities is, all too often, based on its importance as a source of social capital, as a marker of the fact that one has had such an education. To take some contemporary examples, it's the Eton- and Oxford-educated British Foreign Secretary dropping references to the Battle of Marathon, Hercules and Cicero into his speeches, or an Eton- and Oxford-educated Member of the UK Parliament tweeting in Latin: endearing upper-class eccentricity and careless intellectual superiority masking ruthless ambition and disdain for hoi polloi (*never* the solecism of 'the hoi polloi'). It's a private school- and Oxford-educated journalist bemoaning cultural decline because universities have drunk the social justice Kool-Aid and accepted lower-class students onto Classics degree programmes who don't already have the sort of high-level grasp of Latin and Greek that a *proper* education bestows.[16]

This isn't only a concern for the notoriously class-obsessed Brits: in Donna Tartt's *The Secret History* (1992) we are introduced to the Greek class of an exclusive New England liberal arts college as an elite within that elite, a tiny group hand-picked by an eccentric, charismatic teacher to be subjected to his idea of a true education in the classical spirit:

'I believe that having a great diversity of teachers is harmful and confusing for a young mind, in the same way I believe that it is better to know one book intimately than a hundred superficially,' he said. 'I know the modern world tends not to agree with me, but after all, Plato had only one teacher, and Alexander.'[17]

As Richard, the narrator, observes at the end, 'I could say that the secret of Julian's charm was that he latched onto young people who wanted to feel better than everybody else; that he had a strange gift for twisting feelings of inferiority into superiority and arrogance.'[18] Richard himself is a case in point: desperately seeking to be accepted into the group, desperately hoping that his technical skill in language will help mask his humble origins. The lure of Greek culture is a form of cultic initiation, a conviction of one's freedom from modern laws and conventions, as the Greeks show what it means to be truly, authentically human – the epitomes of reason, who also stand for the joyful embrace of unreason. The students' wish to *become* ancients leads them first to re-create ancient religious rites and thence to murder, suicide and incest – and their teacher, when he learns something of events, simply departs on indefinite leave of absence without explanation. The survivors are left confused, damaged – and yet still clearly convinced that, with the break-up of the group and the loss of their mentor, they have lost something vital, not least their own sense of special-ness and exclusivity.

The counterpoint of classical knowledge, however superficial it may be, as a social marker is its role as a means of exclusion; often it comes to be seen as the rightful possession of a single class, race and/ or gender, something that is reinforced at all levels by the expectation that only the extensive study of classical languages at the right sort of school can properly equip someone for a full engagement with the classics at university. Classics both confers and depends on elite status: just as, for the ancients, only those able to afford a life of leisure could become properly developed human beings in the eyes of their fellow elites, so only those with a 'proper' elite education can become proper classicists today.

Classics has never been a completely closed shop: there is a long tradition of autodidacts, acquiring knowledge of antiquity through their own efforts (and through the wonders of public libraries and organizations like the Workers' Educational Association) – sometimes seeking to join the clas-sical elite on its own terms and to be accepted as proper classicists despite their disadvantages, sometimes – more rarely – seeking to turn classical knowledge to more radical ends and to reclaim it for a wider section of the population. In post-war Britain, this was often bound up with the grammar school system, creaming off a small proportion of the brightest lower-class children in order to initiate them into the ways of the higher culture; entry into relative privilege and expanded opportunities for the chosen few, including the chance to study classics, at the expense of condemning the majority to a much cheaper, basically unacademic education. Not that it was wholly wonderful for the chosen few: one of them, the poet Tony Harrison, in 'Classics Society' (1978), dramatizes the experience of being caught between different worlds, with Latin symbolizing the loss of the language of his parents and former friends:

> We boys can take old Hansards and translate
> the British Empire into SPQR
> but nothing too demotic or too up-to-date,
> and *not* the English that I speak at home. . . .[19]

Harrison presents the problematic nature of classical knowledge in Britain in the 1950s: taught as a sterile end in itself, as a marker of separation between classes and their destined roles in society (and, less emphasized in his poems, the fact that it is above all *boys* who are offered such an education).

For all the inspiration Harrison has drawn from classical literature throughout his writing career, including reworkings of Greek tragedy and a drama, *The Trackers of Oxyrhynchus* (1988), explicitly focused on the clashes within the modern recovery of antiquity between high and low culture, refined classicizing speech and the vulgar vernacular, it remains a source of personal and artistic tension. Classics offers a possible route from one world into another, at the expense of reinforcing its association with social superiority and elitism. It is far harder to travel in the opposite direction, making classical knowledge accessible to everyone, when the discipline of classics maintains its gatekeeping role and insists on the primacy of high-level linguistic and philological knowledge as a prerequisite for proper engagement with classical antiquity.

#NotAllClassicists

Classical knowledge as cultural capital, as a mark of superiority over the lower classes, over women (the majority of whom were judged incapable of appreciating it) and over the barbarous natives. Classical knowledge as a source of smugness and arrogance – and of precedents for such an attitude, in the writings of the Greeks and Romans themselves. Classical knowledge as proudly detached from the world, as the mark of a proper gentleman (or at least of someone willing to pretend to that status by adopting its manners and assumptions). Classical knowledge as a weapon in the culture wars and the clash of civilizations, as the basis for claims about the innate superiority of the genetic heirs of the European tradition. Classics as a symbol of 'white resistance' to multiculturalism, in far-right internet memes and the adoption of supposedly Spartan symbols; classics as the foundation of traditional values, so that their decline in American schools is seen as the source of hysteria, censorship, moral relativism and, as one online article argued, 'a generation of gender-bending freaks'.[20]

From this perspective, classics in the twenty-first century matters because it is dangerous and pernicious. Classics denies, or at least downgrades, the claims of any other global culture to be valued and taken seriously; it elevates a set of narrow technical skills as the core of 'education'; it reinforces hierarchies of race, gender and class, providing ideological cover for western imperialism in multiple forms and for different versions of white supremacy, while entirely failing to live up to its occasional grandiose claims about producing better, more humane and cultivated people. Knowledge of classical antiquity and its products, and their enormous weight of inherited prestige and authority, is put to dangerous, divisive and destructive ends; and classics as a discipline prefers to ensure its own survival by aiding and abetting the over-valuation of the classical world and its culture, rather than rejecting such appropriation.

This picture is, of course, one-sided and unfair, and my academic colleagues will rightly protest about it. In the first place, it has been classicists themselves (some of them, anyway) who have been at the forefront of questioning traditional understanding of the classical world and how it should be studied, analysing the ways in which ideas about classical antiquity have been used and abused by later centuries, and holding up a mirror to the practices and assumptions of their own discipline, including its patchy track record in contributing to a fairer, more equal society. The fiercest critiques of the idealization of Greece and Rome as pinnacles of human civilization have come from classicists, pointing instead to the way those societies were founded on violence, slavery and misogyny – even at the risk of undermining one of the justifications for the survival of classics as a discipline, namely the inherited prestige of its subject matter. As we will see in subsequent chapters, the idea that classics is dedicated to the perpetuation of an idealized vision of Greece and Rome as the foundations of 'Western Civilization', and to the rote learning of language skills to the exclusion of all other forms of scholarly work, is decades out of date – for all that it suits some non-classicists (and, to be fair, certain classics graduates) to paint such a picture of it.

The classical world and its cultural products are *not* inherently allied to the agendas of western imperialism, white supremacism, fascism or anti-Islamism, even if that is often claimed by those pushing such agendas, and even if classicists could sometimes be rather louder in their condemnation of these attempts. The study of the ancient world – even when this is done in a traditional philological manner – is not intrinsically elitist, any more than the study of the literature, history and culture of any other society is. It is of course easier, for a variety of reasons, for people from relatively privileged backgrounds to take the risk of studying a non-vocational humanities subject, and the particular importance given to the classical languages (and the question of who has access to them before university) certainly plays a part in attracting certain kinds of students (some of whom go on to become the next generation of teachers) and deterring others. Classics as a discipline, in Europe and America, remains extremely white and very middle class, despite the fact that the balance between the sexes at all but the highest professorial levels has become more even in recent decades. It is sometimes argued that these imbalances reflect the demography of the students who choose to study classical subjects, and that things are gradually changing – but there is much more to be done to counter the effects of several centuries of classics presenting itself as proudly elitist, male and white, not least by emphasizing the proud but often overlooked tradition of working-class, female and non-white classicists and their efforts to offer alternative perspectives on the subject.

One might argue that classics, as a discipline, has been the victim of its own success. Classics managed to establish itself in schools and universities through the cultural importance of its subject matter and through claims about the excellence and difficulty of its technical skills, as well as the fact that the existence of such a discipline, precisely because of its elite status, was useful for other purposes. While masquerading as a pedigree animal, it was always, in reality, a mongrel – fighting for territory with other, larger and more popular disciplines, scavenging methods and ideas from wherever it could find them, peopled by eccentrics and obsessives who were regarded with contempt by some of those they taught. The cultural image of classics and classicists as elite and superior, which always risks it appearing irrelevant and pedantic, has never been more than partly true, a manoeuvre to ensure the survival of the subject by those whose basic dedication was to the intrinsic interest of the literature, culture and history of the ancient world. Today, its methods and ideas are more varied than ever. It is constantly threatened with dissolution into other disciplines, as ancient historians pay more attention to their fellow historians than to what the classical literature people are doing, as classical philosophers look to mainstream philosophy rather than to art and archaeology, and so forth. What holds it together is a shared commitment to the investigation of the societies of classical antiquity, not because they are thought to be intrinsically superior or more essential for 'Western Civilization' than other societies, but simply because these different scholars have all developed an interest in this fascinating topic rather than another.

The past matters, and continues to matter, to the present, in multiple ways; therefore an accurate knowledge of the past, in all its facets, is important, and likewise an understanding of how that past has come to matter, how it has been interpreted and misunderstood and manipulated over the centuries. Classical antiquity remains an important part of the past that matters in Europe and North America; in its actual impact on the development of present-day societies, and in its continuing role as a powerful cultural idea, even a myth. Contrary to long-standing assumptions, it is not true that everyone should have a rich knowledge of ancient Greece and Rome, let alone that this is all one really needs to know – classical antiquity is only one of the traditions that informs our present. But we do need people who know classical antiquity, who can compare it with other historical periods and cultural traditions, explore how it has shaped the present (for good and ill), and chart ways in which our societies can draw positive inspiration from it for the future. The place of classical antiquity in the modern world remains deeply problematic – and that is precisely why classics still matters. Whatever some of my more traditional colleagues may think, I come not to bury classics but to praise it . . .

2

Charting the Past

Boundaries

The basic goal of classical studies is the reconstruction of entire worlds, in all their different aspects. That may seem a slightly odd way of putting it – surely the focus of the discipline is on the recovery of a single world, that of classical Greece and Rome? But one of the main insights of centuries of research in this field has been that there are always different perspectives, different points of focus and different time frames; any single perspective, ancient or modern, is always going to be partial and misleading, whatever its aspirations to completeness – and most scholars, at any one time, are working on more detailed bits of the picture rather than attempting a grand overview. There are fundamental disagreements even about whether we can or should talk in

41

general terms about 'classical antiquity', or draw a clear distinction between Greece and Rome, or break the subject down into even smaller components. Different approaches make more or less sense for different topics: economic historians are more likely to talk about 'the ancient economy' because it appears, especially when compared to later periods, to be fairly homogeneous, while cultural historians tend to emphasize the significant differences between Greece, Rome and other ancient societies. This isn't a universal practice: there are also plenty of economic historians who see significant variation over space and time and so would be wary of generalizing about 'the ancient economy', while some cultural historians trace common themes and ideas – the idea of the Monster and the monstrous in myth and literature, for example – across centuries of classical culture. These differences and arguments are central to the discipline. Of course, classics is all about the accumulation of knowledge and understanding, but it's also about the confrontation of and negotiation between different perceptions and perspectives. It's about the different aspects of life in the ancient world and its continuing legacy, and the different ways we have of studying and interpreting them.

Academic disciplines have always tended to draw boundaries and establish definitions in order to mark off 'their' territory and defend it against other disciplines. Classics today takes a different approach, which one could say reflects its subject matter: antiquity was not a world where fixed, impermeable boundaries played a significant role, and even the frontiers of the later Roman Empire, which we tend to think of in terms of Hadrian's Wall or some other fiercely guarded fortification, were more like zones of contact and supervised movement. People, goods and ideas were constantly on the move, with only intermittent concern for political boundaries – which changed dramatically over the centuries. We can take a snapshot of this world at any given point, and divide it up between different states or cultural groups, and even draw some sort of line between 'the classical world' and everything else – but we know that's an artificial exercise, and that things will rapidly change once history is set in motion again. In the same way, we can look at the current activity of people working in the field of classical studies (many of whom wouldn't necessarily call themselves classicists); we could map their chosen research focus onto axes of geography and chronology, and identify clear hotspots in certain regions at certain times – a definite preference for Greece and Italy, a clear drift towards the fifth to fourth centuries BCE in the former case and the second century BCE to the fourth century CE in the latter. But such a map of activity is not the same as saying that these are the set boundaries of the discipline in any essential sense; they reflect a variety of factors, including the availability of different sorts of evidence, traditions of research and external pressures like student demand and public interest. Classics no longer seeks to define itself in terms of an exclusive right to interpret a limited, supposedly superior body of material; it aspires rather to be an open discipline, a meeting point for different perspectives – an *agora*, the central space of a Greek city, where people met for trade, politics and friendship, rather than a fortified acropolis.

Above all, this is because classicists have an ever clearer sense of how their chosen worlds fit into a wider universe, and how trying to study them in isolation is always a hopeless (or dangerously misleading) enterprise. Take geography. There is certainly a substantial focus on the world of the Mediterranean, partly because of the special importance of Greece and Rome in the tradition of classical studies, partly because – from certain perspectives – the Mediterranean itself and its environment are important, shaping the development of societies around its shores and in drawing them together into a single connected space. It's occasionally suggested that classics (or at any rate the more historical elements) might be renamed 'Ancient Mediterranean Studies' for this reason. But classicists regularly look further east, not only because of specific events (the Persian invasion of Greece at one end of ancient history, the incursions of Eurasian tribes into the Roman Empire at the other), but also because of the constant flow of goods and ideas backwards and forwards, from near eastern influences on early Greek culture or later Roman religion, to the spread of Greek culture through Persia and beyond. This is often interpreted in terms of contacts between 'the Mediterranean world' (as our primary focus) and exterior forces; but it's equally possible, and increasingly productive, to switch perspectives, and see the Mediterranean as the western extremity of Eurasia – the Med as the far end of complex trans-continental trade networks rather than at the centre of things, or the Greek *polis* (the independent 'city state') not as a unique European invention but as one version of a near eastern phenomenon. We are increasingly conscious of how far our traditional perspective was shaped by the ideas of the Greeks themselves, who insisted – in the face of substantial evidence – that every non-Greek was slavish and uncivilized, a mere babbler ('barbarian'). In a similar manner, when northern Europe comes into the picture with the expansion of cultural exchange and Roman conquest, we have learnt to think in terms of what the 'natives' got out of the adoption of 'Roman culture' – and how far they contributed to the development of the idea of what it was to be Roman – rather than seeing everything from the Roman perspective as the dissemination of true civilization to savages.

Classics certainly has a tendency to focus on some regions more than others: Greece and Italy, above all (and, when it comes to the Roman period, a remarkable degree of attention paid to the rather marginal province of Britain, for obvious historical reasons). But even this isn't entirely simple. Where is 'Greece'? Round the Aegean Sea, including the coast of Turkey; in colonies all around the Mediterranean and Black Sea, across in Iran and Afghanistan after the dramatic conquests of Alexandria, and in Argentina and Malibu once we start considering later receptions and the movement of objects. 'Rome', meanwhile, comes to encompass most of Europe – and then, as the archetypal image of imperial power, to conquer regions that were never part of its actual empire (think of the Roman-style triumphal arches to be found in places like Berlin and New York). Other cultures within the same geographical space have, traditionally, been studied in terms of their relations to one or other of these two, often in the role of enemies (the Carthaginians, most obviously, but also the Celts); but they are increasingly studied in their own right, or as part of wider systems of international relations, trade or ecology. It's undeniably true that many classicists should get out more and remember that Rome wasn't just Rome or even Italy, that they're investigating a world where the idea of 'Rome' and 'Roman' was constantly being negotiated and reinvented, rather than a fixed point around which one can construct an academic enterprise. But the traditional idea of the exceptional nature of certain regions of the Mediterranean, the idea that only they are really worth studying, is increasingly recognized as a problematic illusion or ideological assertion. The Mediterranean offers a centre of gravity to the discipline, so to speak, not a geographical boundary.

The same is true of chronology. When was Rome? The Roman Empire never ended; it had (and has) a continuing life in many of the underlying structures and cultures of Europe, and an enduring influence as the archetypal empire – there isn't an obvious end point to studying it. Of course, we can again discern a certain pattern in the amount of attention paid to different periods: the Greek city state (especially, if not solely, Athens and Sparta), the Roman Republic and Empire, followed by late antiquity (admittedly with a continuing tendency to assume that the fall of Rome in the West in the fifth century CE marks the end of our interest, rather than the ongoing Roman Empire in the east), and the Hellenistic Kingdoms (not just the ever-popular Alexander). But again these are patterns of scholarly activity, driven partly by external forces rather than a conviction that these periods are somehow superior. There is plenty of research at the outer chronological reaches, problematizing the question of when (if at all) we can usefully think of the 'classical world' starting. The history of Greek culture extends back into the eighth century BCE and beyond, with Homer and the influences from near eastern societies on the religion, mythology and art of the Aegean. Going further back, the societies of the Bronze Age, the Mycenaeans and Minoans, are largely in the hands of archaeologists rather than other kinds of scholars, but that doesn't mark a clear division from classical studies – not least because analysis of Linear B, the language used in the Mycenaean palaces for record-keeping, reveals a clear connection to later Greek. At the other end of 'classical history' as commonly understood, the sole point of agreement is that the traditional closing date of 476 CE, the removal of the last Roman emperor in the West, is completely unhelpful. There is no abrupt break in continuity to be located, even in politics – power had long since shifted away from the emperors to a new political-military elite, the emperor in the east continued to insist on his prerogatives, much of the administrative structure remained in place – while in other areas of life this symbolic change had little or no effect. The transition from 'ancient' to 'early medieval' history is more or less seamless, even if specialists in the field may find themselves in different university departments from their colleagues.

Geographical and chronological boundaries are always artificial: states draw lines on a map, historians divide up time into centuries or eras, and both then expect that these distinctions should be significant. Political historians – modern as well as ancient – have a tendency to assume that political changes will always mark major ruptures (in classical studies, the key example is the claim that the rise of Augustus as the first emperor must have been felt in every area of Roman life). Social and economic historians, on the other hand, see changes following quite different rhythms and timescales; likewise, scholars studying the development of thought, or poetry, or sculpture, or architecture. Different perspectives define their field of study and organize their material in different ways. Perhaps because classical studies has always involved this multitude of perspectives, it's impossible to avoid exploring the relationships and clashes between them: political narratives are confronted with literary ones; the spaces of economic activity are compared with those of artistic styles; certain aspects of the worlds of antiquity are isolated, explored in depth, and then we argue about how to reconcile them with the wider picture.

Often, this exchange between different scholarly perspectives and different geographical and temporal frames is the source of the most exciting new research questions. How did the expansion of Roman political control through Italy affect the languages spoken in different regions and how did Italian multilingualism affect that expansion? How did the expansion of 'Hellenic' culture into Asia change ideas of what that culture meant? Above all, it constantly emphasizes the gaps and discrepancies between our ideas of 'classical culture' and 'the ancient world' – which we all tend to have, as a kind of working hypothesis or assumption – and the realities that we find in the evidence. 'The classical world' is a construct – part ancient, part modern – one interpretation of a world that was complex and fluid. Classics doesn't attempt to draw a line around this imaginary object and claim it for its own; it takes the inherited ideas of 'the classical' as a starting point and opens them up to debate.

Absences

The basic condition of studying pretty well any aspect of classical antiquity is the shortage of evidence, and hence the limitations and uncertainties of our knowledge. This is partly just the effect of the passage of time. Things decay – even modern books are falling apart as their paper deteriorates or the ink fades. It's scarcely a wonder, therefore, that organic materials from the past have tended to perish, unless they're preserved in the most favourable conditions (arid deserts or oxygen-free bogs, so that the growth of destructive microbes is inhibited). This loss robs us not only of potential evidence in the materials themselves, but, when it comes to texts, also of what was written on them. Inorganic materials like stone and pottery do rather better, though metals may be melted down and reused; but there are limits to what pottery can tell us about life in antiquity, and we are all too conscious, rejoicing in the survival of inscriptions, that it was the wealthy who were most likely to invest in posterity by having their actions and identities chiselled into stone, as well as most likely to enjoy the possession of objects that could survive for generations. In brief, classicists are constantly aware of the effects of time in destroying so much of what once existed, which we could have used; we may look with envy to the wealth enjoyed by researchers in other periods, such as copious private papers and diaries, or the complete notes and jottings of a poet rather than just his published works, or the correspondence between two philosophers. We are mindful that what has survived is not necessarily representative of all the inhabitants of antiquity or of every region or every period. We seek to take somewhere like Vindolanda, the Roman fort by Hadrian's Wall, as a microcosm, crossing our fingers that the miraculously preserved everyday objects (Roman shoes!) and the personal letters can be taken as evidence for life across the whole Roman Empire rather than being specific to life on the northern frontier of the northernmost province. We can often make a pretty good case for this – but we would still much rather have more material, from many other places.

It isn't only time that has thinned out the material we have to work with; at least as destructive, and perhaps even more damaging, is selection by people. Some things survived because someone made an effort to try to preserve them, by putting documents or coins in a container and burying it, or by carefully interring goods in a tomb. Plenty of objects survived only by chance, and we can only imagine how much else was simply discarded. The most obvious example is texts, most of which survive only in copies – the originals would long since have perished – because someone thought they were worth copying and re-copying over the centuries. This cost time and money; not every text was thought to be worth copying, or copied in sufficient quantities to increase the chances of it surviving into the early modern period and being recovered by scholars; and it is clear that ideas about *which* texts were worth preserving changed over time, with different judgements about value and usefulness. Even some plays by the three great Athenian tragic playwrights, acknowledged at the time as pinnacles of literature, survive only as fragments of scenes or individual lines, or even just as titles; we have virtually nothing left of Athenian Old Comedy apart from Aristophanes, and not all of him. If we read the works of the Roman agricultural writers, they offer copious lists of their sources, including Carthaginian as well as Greek authors – which now survive only in these bibliographies. The ideas of many early philosophers are known just because later ones quoted them, taking their words out of context and incorporating them into what may have been quite different arguments.

The most notorious and important cases of this process of selection are found in late antiquity, where Christians selected certain earlier authors as worthy of copying and discarded others as godless, immoral or simply irrelevant to their interests. In the same period, non-Christians were producing compilations of extracts and quotes from earlier texts, anthologies of wisdom and insight that unfortunately went hand in hand with the neglect of the full versions of the originals. It's not that every text that was copied at this time necessarily survived, but its chances were clearly improved. Other texts could still survive, whether as papyrus fragments in the arid deserts of Egypt, or papyrus strips recycled as mummy wrappings, or pieces of parchment being reused for a new work, with the original still readable 'between the lines' (the stinginess of ancient copyists, or maybe just the high cost of new parchment, has been an enormous boon). But the basic situation is that we know we have only a tiny proportion of everything ever written in antiquity, even of its finest literary and intellectual products, let alone of more mundane material – and we know that what we have is *not* a random sample.

This possible bias – that is to say, we know the process as a whole was not entirely random, but we can't be certain in any particular case – has at times also been fuelled by the activities of modern scholars and lovers of the classics. For centuries, the focus on Greece and Rome in terms of their cultural glories meant that this was what people tended to look for – literature and philosophy from the most important ancient writers rather than farming manuals or guides to Roman plumbing – and there is still a tendency to emphasize some kinds of texts over others. It's even more obvious when it comes to material evidence, where for centuries activity concentrated on the recovery of works of 'art' and monumental buildings rather than evidence of more humble lives; we still know vastly more about the temples and palaces of the city of Rome than about its high-rise apartment buildings. The antiquarian spirit and the mania for all things classical meant that in some cases everything would be preserved simply because of its antiquity – the contents of country museums in Britain and France stand witness to this – though the focus on 'objects' means we may lack proper context for the finds.

What we have is only a small sample. We draw tentative conclusions on the basis of what has survived, in full knowledge that our interpretations might have been different if we had more or different evidence. We constantly face the question of whether the absence of evidence, or at least the very small amounts of evidence, can be taken as evidence of absence. How far did the Roman state keep detailed records of its activities? How far did businessmen maintain careful accounts rather than just operating by rules of thumb? When we see a fall in the number of shipwrecks in the Mediterranean from the second century CE, does this represent a fall in the number of sea voyages and a decline in the level of economic activity – or is it just a function of which shipwrecks were most likely to be found? Classicists spend much of their time debating uncertainties and evaluating the relative plausibility of different interpretations, rather than being able to offer hard-and-fast, yes-or-no answers to questions about what the ancient world was like – which can be a serious problem when engaging with a wider non-academic world, where scholarly caution, not going beyond what the evidence can plausibly support, looks like equivocation or ignorance. But there's no alternative.

There is always a risk of concluding that we cannot say anything much, or at least giving that impression; there's always a risk in the other direction of allowing our view of antiquity to be shaped by what has been preserved, as if it is wholly representative of what once existed. However, it's also possible to be too pessimistic about this. New evidence continues to be found, sometimes in remarkable quantities – the continuing discovery and publication of papyri, for example, with a fabulous mixture of literary passages, often originally used for school exercises, and utterly mundane (but to a historian fascinating) documents like census returns and private legal contracts. New scientific techniques create new opportunities: the 'virtual unrolling' of carbonized papyrus rolls from Herculaneum so that the writing can be deciphered without having to open or destroy the object (though this does create conditions for conflict between scholars who want more texts to work with and archaeologists who want to focus on preserving remains that have already been excavated rather than digging up more buildings). New questions about the past support a search for new sorts of evidence; new scientific techniques prompt new questions: for example, the analysis of cores extracted from the Greenland ice sheet enables us to get a sense not only of changing global temperatures (was there a 'Roman Warm Period' that aided the empire's expansion, and/or a cooling in late antiquity that contributed to undermining Roman society?) but also of changing patterns of human activity, with trace elements in the atmosphere pointing to an expansion in metal production and pollution. With the power of modern computing, we can create databases of texts or inscriptions and search them for patterns, reconstruct buildings and even chart Mediterranean sailing routes on the basis of weather data, navigation software and our knowledge of the sailing capacities of ancient ships.

None of this evidence offers simple answers; scientific data, like everything else we work with, has to be interrogated and interpreted. We don't pretend to be able to do the analysis better than the specialists, but we can ask questions about the ways the analysis was framed and the results were interpreted. For example, we have a wide range of different kinds of evidence, both textual and material, pointing to the presence of people of a wide range of ethnic backgrounds and geographical origins in Roman Britain, while a study of the DNA of a sample of the modern British population doesn't show much trace of 'African' heritage. Rather than rejecting the former findings because the latter is more 'scientific', classicists explore the relative plausibility of each form of analysis, and raise questions about whether the genetic studies actually show, or are capable of showing, what some people claim they do.[1] Classicists are experts in considering as many different sorts of evidence as possible, because we virtually never have enough of any of it – and of negotiating and understanding the inevitable inconsistences and contradictions that we find. We are – because we have to be – professionally sceptical and cautious, aware of the tentative nature of any interpretation.

Approaches

We can also celebrate the long tradition of classicists taking advantage of their disadvantages: responding to the limitations of evidence by becoming ever more imaginative in how to go about interpreting it. Not every classical scholar does this, but as a discipline we can never afford to be introverted, relying wholly on our own intellectual resources and traditional practices; rather, most classicists are constantly eavesdropping on what's going on in other disciplines, listening out both for new questions and for new ideas about how we might read our evidence. This occasionally leads to accusations of anachronism, that we 'impose' modern ideas on a non-modern past – and it's true that this is always a possibility. But any attempt at studying the past, certainly any past that is more distant than a decade or so, is inevitably anachronistic; we see it with the benefit of hindsight, knowing what happened next, and we translate it into our own idiom, relying on our own preconceived assumptions, concepts and priorities. Drawing more explicitly on modern ideas and theories, conscious that we are reading the past in present terms, is less rather than more likely to give us a misleading impression. It offers a means of deepening understanding, by suggesting new research questions and new ways of looking at the familiar evidence – and even of creating new areas of research altogether.

To take just one important example, we can chart the influence of feminism and modern understandings of gender in improving our understanding of the past. Until the late 1960s, women were scarcely recognized as objects of scholarly investigation – at best, we find passing discussion of them as the objects of poetic desire or mythological misfortune, or prurient accounts of the very rare cases where they took on roles in the normally male world of politics and war, like Cleopatra or Boudicca – and this was certainly not regarded as a problem by those studying antiquity. The development of feminist ideas directed scholars' attention to the place of women within the structures of society and culture as an essential research question – the basic tenet of this body of thought, one could say, was that 'women' should be a significant term of social analysis – in the past as well as in the present. This created a whole new area of research, seeking to reconstruct the lives of ancient women in general, not just a few exceptional examples, and to understand how far and in what ways ancient societies rested on their control and exploitation. These pioneering attempts highlighted the limitations of the evidence, which now, for the first time, was explicitly identified and labelled as predominantly male in authorship and audience, rather than this being taking for granted as unproblematic. Recognizing the source problem emphasized the difficulty of recovering the reality of women's lives, let alone their thoughts and feelings, as opposed to male representations of them – were Athenian women *really* confined in seclusion in one corner of the house, or is that a male ideal or a solely elite practice? – but it also at least provided a sense of what we don't know but wish we did, of the partial nature of our image of antiquity. We can now recognize significant absences both in our sources and in modern reconstructions and assumptions: how the woman's contribution to the Greek household, depicted, for example, in Xenophon's *Oikonomikos*, is presented in certain ways within a specifically male philosophical discourse, and then interpreted differently by modern historians with a fixation on 'proper' (i.e. male) productive labour.

The later development of theories of gender, as the cultural expression of sexual difference and of expectations of the appropriate behaviour of men and women, expanded the range of ancient evidence that could be considered. Rather than ignoring a satirist like Juvenal, on the basis that he manifestly doesn't provide evidence about the lives of actual women, we can read him as a reflection of and/or upon the prejudices of Roman patriarchy, of the interdependent conceptions of masculinity and femininity. Some studies aim primarily at reconstructing the past as an end in itself; others are more explicitly political and ambitious in their intent, not just putting women back into the historical picture (where there's a risk that women's history just becomes a minor sub-field, to be covered in a section or a chapter of more general books and then ignored) but rethinking our whole understanding. How far should we characterize Greek or Roman society as patriarchal, exploring how its whole structure rested on the marginalization and control of women, or see classical culture as essentially misogynistic, from the innumerable rape stories in classical mythology, celebrated by poets and artists, to the depiction of women as uncontrolled, bestial creatures and sources of corruption found in ancient thought, satire and early Christian writings? Feminism and gender don't just offer a new field of investigation, they push us to re-evaluate everything we thought we knew.

This is manifestly a modern perspective. The Greeks and Romans certainly thought in terms of the differences between the sexes, and had established norms of sexual behaviour and stereotypes – though, it should be stressed, these were not identical with ours – but they didn't analyse them in terms of 'gender' or 'patriarchy'. There are fascinating examples of ancient attempts at exploring what we would call gender issues – it's one of the great things about the Greeks and Romans that some of them were happy to critically examine every aspect of their lives from the ground up – for example in the Attic tragedies (the powerful figures of Antigone, Medea or Hecuba, articulating criticism of the male world and its values at whose hands they suffer) or comedy (Aristophanes exploring the possibilities of an assembly taken over by women in *Assemblywomen* or a sex strike against war as a means of questioning the norms of society in *Lysistrata*). For the most part, however, ancient authors accepted the traditional norms as, well, normal and unquestioned, and an uncritical reading of their writings wouldn't alert us to anything worth discussing. It's the idea of gender that helps us to recognize these issues and enriches our understanding of the past.

This is never a matter of simply imposing modern ideas on the past; the anachronism lies in the fact that we cannot avoid making sense of the past in our own terms. Often, the result of analysing antiquity through these modern ideas is to emphasize differences as much as similarity; the conscious use of concepts and theoretical ideas compels us to be explicit about how we are interpreting the evidence, rather than offering our interpretations as if they are obvious common sense. Take the example of ethnicity. Modern accounts of antiquity have, until quite recently, taken it for granted that the Greeks and Romans were unproblematically and monolithically 'white' (see, for instance, illustrations in popular history books and Latin textbooks). The occasional depictions or descriptions of 'Ethiopians' or other Africans in ancient texts or mosaics, if remarked upon at all, could be taken as evidence that the ancients saw race in much the same way as later Europeans – or that they saw racial difference, but did not apply the full set of assumptions of natural inferiority that the nineteenth century did.

The explicit and theoretically informed study of ancient ethnicity, of how physical and cultural differences were marked and interpreted in antiquity and how conceptions of self and other were constructed, makes it clear that either approach is hopelessly simplistic; it's the modern notion of 'whiteness', and the assumption that this basically equates to Hellenic or Roman identity, that is the anachronism. The theory sets up a dialogue between past and present, exploring the differences and similarities – and highlighting how far our understanding, whether of past or present, is shaped by our concepts and assumptions.

There are modern theories that make stronger claims about their universal applicability, and hence the irrelevance of historical difference: neoclassical economics is an obvious example, or evolutionary psychology. The instincts of the typical classicist revolt against grand assertions about universal human nature, insisting on the importance of cultural difference – but we recognize at the same time the explanatory power of such a theory, *if* we can be persuaded of its validity. This question therefore becomes a focus of debate, exploring both the theory itself and the plausibility of accounts of the ancient world which take it as a starting point. Texts and other evidence can always be interpreted in different ways, and so you *can* read the Roman economists in terms of rational choice theory, or Virgil's *Aeneid* through Freudian psychoanalysis (all those parental issues . . .); the question is always whether such readings appear more or less persuasive or productive. We might object to the political implications of assuming that modern economic theory expresses a universal truth (certainly someone like Karl Marx would vigorously object, insisting that antiquity was not in any way capitalist) – but the opposite position is equally political, seeking to establish antiquity as a safe space from capitalism. It's always political, it's always a matter of competing interpretations; and it's theory that enables such debates.

Classicists tend to be magpies, looking for useful ideas in any relevant area of study – exploring current developments in cognitive science, for example, as a basis for considering how late antique sermons were constructed to persuade listeners to change their behaviour, or reading up on media theory to explore how ancient states developed their images and established their legitimacy, or adopting a bit of network theory to interpret ancient trade and migration, or looking to anthropology, or comparative literature, or philosophy, or political science. This habit always runs the risks of amateurism, of being out of date and/or having only a superficial understanding – the vice of reading a couple of books rather than immersing oneself fully in the subject, when acquiring a fuller knowledge might require a greater investment of time than the potential reward justifies. We are busy enough trying to stay on top of the latest research in our own field, let alone trying to familiarize ourselves with what's going on in another, and there are plenty of examples of ancient economic historians having a terrible grasp of economics and the like. More and more, the answer to this problem is not a retreat back to a safe disciplinary space, but collaboration and intellectual exchange: classical scholars working with those in other fields, learning one another's language (the technical vocabulary, but still more the taken-for-granted assumptions of each discipline), and seeking to ensure that the resultant research will be credible and interesting to those in the other field, not just to fellow classicists. The future is comparative – and of course that applies still more strongly within the discipline, itself the original interdisciplinary field of study, where archaeologists rub shoulders with linguists, philosophers with art historians, literature specialists with economic historians.

Languages

At this point, if not long since, you may be asking: but isn't classics all about the languages? Greek and Latin, of course, and maybe Hebrew or Aramaic or Sanskrit, or Old Persian or Egyptian and Coptic, or Gothic, or Arabic – but definitely Greek and Latin? Traditionally, as discussed in the first chapter, linguistic and philological skills were indeed seen as the heart of the entire classical enterprise, the training that set classicists apart from other disciplines and gave them full, unmediated access to the wonders of classical civilization. Becoming a classicist meant becoming a skilled reader of classical texts in the original language; one might then continue with philological research, recovering, correcting and completing texts and analysing their language in detail, or instead turn such linguistic skills to the elucidation of literature, or historical or philosophical texts – but always with a thorough grounding in the languages as the indispensable basis for any sort of classical research. Even the investigator of classical architecture, art or material culture might be expected to have an expert command of the ancient languages, in order to understand the texts that could elucidate those objects: ancient treatises on art and architecture, descriptions of different buildings, accounts of ancient life, and so forth.

This reveals an obvious problem with such an approach, useful as language skills undoubtedly are for anyone studying a different culture: insofar as classics had the ambition to offer a complete account of the worlds of classical antiquity, its notion of completeness was narrow and partial, confined to what the texts could reveal – and for the most part only a selection of texts, the central canon defined largely by cultural prestige and perceived literary merit. This tended to lead to a focus on a limited number of Great Works, assumed to be definitive and to contain everything that anyone (apart from specialists) would ever want to know about antiquity, rather than any attempt at reconstructing the whole range of ancient writing and thought – it's an attitude that persists in Great Books courses. With historical topics, this approach led not only to a reliance on what ancient elites had to say about themselves (neglecting the fact that most of the ancient world wasn't directly represented in the surviving texts), but also to a focus on the subjects that ancient elites found interesting – politics and war, rather than economy or society, let alone the lives of the masses. In archaeology, this literary focus tended to define the questions being asked of the material: every site should, if possible, be linked to somewhere named in an ancient text (and often archaeological activity was driven by the search for named sites), every layer of destruction at a site should be connected to a battle known to have taken place in the neighbourhood, and the over-all development of any region was interpreted in terms of the dominant historical, text-based interpretation. For example, decades of archaeological activity in the region around the city of Rome were dedicated to testing the idea that, as set out in a biography written by the second-century CE Greek author Plutarch, the second-century BCE Roman populist politician Tiberius Gracchus had travelled through the area and been horrified to find it deserted. The fact that archaeological surveys found plenty of sites and other activity during this period, rather than a deserted region, had to be explained or explained away, whereas a more self-confident, archaeologically driven research programme would have concentrated on evaluating what the material evidence actually revealed, and then, perhaps, used this as a context for evaluating remarks in the literary sources.[2]

The problem here is not just the impact of such a narrow focus on our understanding of antiquity – that has now largely been resolved by expanding the types of evidence that scholars consider to include, well, everything available, and by expanding the sorts of questions to be considered beyond those suggested by the texts. Classicists today have a far stronger sense of the limitations of those texts, what they can and can't tell us, and far more ways of developing new questions and interpretations. The problem is also the impact on the standing of the discipline in the wider culture, the way that it is seen by others, and as a result the make-up of its students and teachers. As long as 'Proper Classics' is defined in terms of the ancient languages, so that teachers and researchers are expected to have a high-level command of at least one and preferably both, regardless of whether that's actually necessary for their research, the discipline operates a means of exclusion that works against all its other aims. Some schools are more likely than others to teach classical languages to a high level, and hence produce students who feel they could study classics if they wanted to; some types of students are more likely than others to choose classical language study. The creation of 'Classical Studies' programmes at university for students who haven't had the opportunity to study the languages at school doesn't help if such programmes are simply regarded as a weak substitute for the Real Thing. Projects to expand the study of classical subjects in school, wonderful as they are from the perspective of anyone committed to the subject, will only perpetuate the problem if they focus on the teaching of languages alone rather than on the whole range of classical studies.[3]

Classics undoubtedly needs experts in ancient language and literature, those with the depth of knowledge and skill to be able to reconstruct fragmentary texts, appreciate the complexity of their composition, explore metaphors and other literary effects, recognize subtle passing allusions to other works and authors, and so forth. Classics doesn't, however, need everyone to be a linguist. Plenty of areas of classical research can be taken forward, even at the highest level, without needing to read Greek or Latin texts in the original; whether because the evidence for the project is primarily material, or because adequate translations exist, or because the subject matter is actually modern (classical reception, as discussed in the next chapter). Having some knowledge of Latin or Greek is undoubtedly an advantage for studying most topics, so that you can follow the arguments of scholars working on such topics, or make use of a parallel text to check specific points, or check the translation of specific phrases. But it is not necessary for all classical researchers to have the sort of grasp of the language that allows you to work through a text unaided or to teach advanced language to students. It's possible for students to start Greek or Latin at university and develop their skills to a high level, even to match those who've been studying language since the early years of school – but that isn't true of everyone, and we also have to consider what skills they are *not* developing as a result of devoting themselves to language.

The continuing dominance of language in popular ideas of what classics is all about, but also in the assumptions of some professional classicists, is partly a legacy of the history of the discipline, and its claim to special expertise and esoteric knowledge as a means of marking off its territory from other disciplines. But it is also a relic of the tradition of the lone scholar, the idea that all research is done by an individual who therefore needs to have all the necessary skills at their command. This ignores the simple fact that we don't need to do everything ourselves; we can work in collaboration with others, within the discipline as well as outside it. I happen to think that, at least for those working on historical topics, archaeology may be as important as language for a researcher; I therefore work to have enough understanding to make use of the research of specialist archaeologists and to have productive conversations with them. This is normal for most of the different specialisms within classics; it should be normal on the linguistic side as well, so that those researching other fields have enough knowledge of Greek or Latin for working purposes, and if they have a more advanced query they simply go and talk to a specialist.

Contexts

Such promiscuous interdisciplinarity is the key to the success of classics, and to the sheer excitement of working in this field or studying this subject: the discipline incorporates an enormous variety of different perspectives on the classical world, drawing on many different skills and theories, some of which mesh and support one another and some of which are in tension or conflict. Whereas many academic disciplines work largely within a single paradigm, an accepted set of procedures and methodologies, classical studies is about the productive clash of different paradigms, approaches and methodologies. New knowledge and understanding comes from applying new theories to old problems, or drawing on familiar evidence for new problems, or considering different perspectives on the same issue; from a powerful sense that any bit of evidence can be interpreted in multiple ways and in different contexts, which can then be put into productive dialogue with one another.

How should we think about Greek tragedy, to take one of the most central topics of the classical tradition? There are the texts of the plays, first and foremost; the language, the style, the different sorts of poetic meter; there are comparisons to be drawn across the different works of an individual author, and still more between different authors – should we identify a historical development from a more archaic Aeschylus to a sophisticated, 'modern' Euripides, or rather see different writing styles and conceptions of 'the tragic' in dialogue with one another? There are the sources of the plots and characters: the stories found in Greek mythology, the retellings in Homer and other poems, artistic representations on vases or in sculptures – and the ways in which the tragedians adapt this material, altering plots for their own purposes (the version of Oedipus with which we're familiar, besting the Sphinx, marrying his mother and eventually putting out his own eyes, was largely Sophocles' own invention rather than the traditional story). There is the reconstruction of the performance, the way that the play would actually have appeared on the stage, in the specific religious-political context of the great Athenian civic festivals. There are the broader contexts of Athenian or Greek political discourse, assumptions about gender roles, ideas of law or family or community or justice, which sometimes constitute the background to the plays, helping us to interpret the drama, and sometimes are the focus of the whole enterprise. There are the discussions offered by philosophers and critics, the reception of the play by other authors and by visual artists – not to mention modern performances, translations, adaptations, revisions and reworkings, which may in turn influence our interpretation of the original. There are the modern theories of tragedy, of psychology, of political discourse, of media, of theatrical practice, that suggest new questions and readings.

None of these perspectives offers a complete understanding; some of them certainly offer contradictory, or at least incompatible, ideas. They all feed into our debates and discussions about tragedy – and this is just one example of the many worlds and multiple facets of antiquity, just one part of the reconstruction of the past and our understanding of it. Athenian politics is one of the contexts of Attic tragedy, but it's equally true that tragedy is one of the contexts of Athenian politics – we are, after all, dealing with a predominantly oral society, in which speech and performance are key, and we can identify the *agon*, the set-piece debate between two points of view and the struggle to determine meaning, in the theatre and the assembly alike. Partly because of their own interests and partly because that's how the subject is organized, classicists tend to identify themselves with literary studies or historical approaches or philosophy – but time and again it's the breaking down of those barriers, the free exchange of ideas and the exploration of different perspectives on our unavoidably fragmentary knowledge of antiquity, that enables us to chart the past.

3

Understanding the Present

Receiving Antiquity

Classics matters because it has mattered. This is, of course, a subset of why the past in general matters: it tells us, we believe, who we are, what our place is in the world, where our institutions and practices came from. In the case of classics, we are dealing for the most part with imaginary lineages and inheritances, a matter of adoption and adaptation. But it's no less powerful for that.

Innumerable aspects of ancient culture – texts, laws, works of art, ideas, buildings, language, moral examples, clothing – have had a continued effect, long after the demise of the civilizations that produced them. Sometimes we can trace a direct line of continuity from antiquity to the present; more often this tradition has involved the reintroduction of classical remnants that had passed out of common knowledge and usage. Belief in the absolute authority of Greek and Roman models for all fields of culture and knowledge meant that classical ideas came to permeate the cultures of the Renaissance and the early modern period in Europe, and began to spread to other parts of the globe as Europeans headed out on missions of trade and conquest. But this was never a solely European tradition: the Arab world was equally familiar with classical ideas, having incorporated certain Greek texts into its own intellectual culture while medieval Europe, or at least its western parts, knew them only insofar as they were referenced by Latin writers. By the early modern period, educated people across western Europe had an easy familiarity with the classics, and peppered their writings with allusions and references, rarely troubling or needing to provide a reference; and their descendants carried this tradition with them to the Americas, Asia, Africa and the Antipodes. Even as the modern world began to question the absolute authority of the classical, the cultural inheritance of Greece and Rome remained a marvellous storehouse of familiar examples, powerful images and provocative arguments, for philosophers, artists, politicians and historians. In brief, it is difficult to think of any aspect of human culture today, in all but the most determinedly isolated regions, whose past has not in some way been touched by the classical world – even if its contemporary presence in many areas is limited to trace elements.

There really are too many examples to list. Roman law (and some of the pre-Roman elements that fed into it) has influenced the development of law codes across the world, even those based on quite different systems and traditions, such as English common law. Greek and Roman ideas of freedom/liberty appear, on closer inspection, to be radically different from the way they are understood today – but the ideal of classical freedom, and a sense of its importance in antiquity, is an inextricable part of the tradition of discourse that informs our present understanding of politics in the West. Classical figures like Caesar, Cleopatra or Alexander, and the moralizing interpretations of their personalities and actions that already surrounded their biographies in antiquity, remain powerful, complex cultural icons today, their legends regularly refreshed and refigured by dramas, films and television series. The classical column is a ubiquitous feature of buildings across the globe, speaking of dignity and elegance – if also of traditionalism, and even if it has long since become a bit of decoration rather than an essential structural element. The classical is constantly changing, while retaining in many cases a special aura in the eyes of viewers and readers.

The reception of the classical past is always complex and multifarious. To consider just the visual arts: antiquity offered later artists models for direct copying or imitation; a wider sense of how one might (or should) depict the human form; different techniques for working materials like marble or bronze; a set of motifs and attributes that communicate 'classicism'; ancient theoretical writings about art and aesthetics; modern theoretical writings about art and aesthetics drawing on ancient ideas and/or developing new analyses of ancient objects and images; a vast store of potential subject matter (especially mythology and literary versions of mythological stories); evidence of the everyday life of antiquity that could be incorporated into artistic representations (even if ancient cities appear remarkably light and clean, as in the paintings of the nineteenth-century artist Lawrence Alma-Tadema); an impeccable excuse for painting scantily clad women (after all, did the Sirens wear clothes? Herbert James Draper didn't think so [Figure 2]) or for producing outright pornography; ideas of the Greek spirit developed on the basis of studying their art, which could then be used as an inspiration for new art (as in the scholarship of the

Figure 2: Herbert James Draper's *Ulysses and the Sirens* (1909). All in the best possible taste?

great J. J. Winckelmann); and a model of everything that is *wrong* with art against which modernist and avant-garde artists could joyfully rebel – and offer their own, superior versions of classical motifs and the 'true' spirit of antiquity instead, as in Giorgio de Chirico's *The Uncertainty of the Poet* (1913), Salvador Dalí's *Venus de Milo with Drawers* (1936) or Henri Matisse's *Icarus* (1947). In some periods, classical images and the idea of the classical represent artistic perfection, an unattainable ideal, the epitome of beauty and truth; in others, they are a fossil, a dead hand of tradition, a dangerous lie, an object of disgust; often they are both, a focus of debate about the essential qualities and goals of art.

Alternatively, we can survey the multitude of contexts in which a single ancient example has been read and reinterpreted. The fifth-century Athenian writer Thucydides has been a significant authority since his work was reintroduced into western Europe from Byzantium in the fourteenth century. He is often labelled a 'historian', and read not only as a reliable source of information about the events he describes (with many readers perhaps trusting his own claims about his objectivity more than is wise), but also as a model for how history should be researched and written today – even, in the nineteenth century, proclaimed as someone who had established the rules of the new critical 'science of history' that German scholars had only now rediscovered. However, there is an equally long tradition of reading him as a political theorist or philosopher, or some kind of hybrid (the philosopher Thomas Hobbes labelled him 'the most politic historiographer that ever writ', and drew on his ideas about the nature of human society); he is cited as an authority in modern international relations theory (often as the first Realist), in works on strategy and military education and in the curriculum of military academies like the US Naval War College, and in pioneering works of game theory; he features in twentieth-century novels and poetry, in video games, and in the memoirs of Bob Dylan; the words of characters in his account are quoted on war memorials, in Veterans' Day speeches, in the draft constitution of the European Union, and in the US Senate – not least a rather magnificent rap evocation of Pericles' Funeral Oration by Congressman Major Owens in the aftermath of 9/11:

> For all the hijacked years
> Cry rivers,
> Feel the death chill
> Iceberg of frozen
> Bloody tears;
> Defiant orations of Pericles
> Must now rise
> Out of the ashes
> Jefferson's profound principles
> Will outlive the crashes. . . .[1]

These interpretations of Thucydides are inconsistent, and sometimes contradictory; we encounter different Thucydideses in different contexts. But this doesn't seem to affect his standing, just as the image of Thucydides as a writer worth engaging with and citing is constantly reinforced every time that someone on Twitter posts 'History is philosophy teaching by examples: Thucydides' or 'The society that separates its scholars from its warriors will have its thinking done by cowards and its fighting by fools: Thucydides' – neither of which are actually Thucydides' own words.

Such misattributions remind us that much of the time the connection between an instance of classical reception and the reality of classical antiquity may be extremely loose or largely imaginary – without that necessarily reducing the power of the *imagined* past. The classical world and its culture still carry substantial authority, and so part of the task of the classicist may be to point out that this authority is being ascribed to a fiction or a fake. However, it's also worth keeping in mind that classicists may get far too worked up about such things (yes, I speak as someone who runs a Twitter account dedicated to correcting fake Thucydides quotations), insisting on their exclusive right to dictate how the ancient world may be used but also drastically over-valuing the classical element. As practitioners of a beleaguered and marginalized discipline, we are generally delighted to come across classical references in television shows (*Doctor Who* in Pompeii!) or public discourse (Steve

Bannon likes Sparta!) – yes, we are still relevant! – without necessarily thinking them through or considering them objectively. There are examples of research on classical reception that simply describe the classical elements of some modern cultural product, and perhaps identify its ancient antecedents, without any attempt at analysing their effect or considering the text or artwork in its more immediate contexts. We automatically identify the classical aspects, and assume that they must be just as obvious to others – and just as important. In fact, most aspects of modern international relations theory, and certainly its core tenets and assumptions, would be unaffected by the removal of all references to Thucydides. That's not to say that Thucydides isn't important at all (the fact that IR theorists won't stop citing him, even when articles are published telling them they should, is a sign of *something*) – but he's certainly not as important to that discipline as he is to classicists identifying references to him.

Indeed, there's a case that classicists may not necessarily be the best people to study classical reception; we have an intimate knowledge of the ancient original, but as a result we tend to exaggerate its importance and ignore the extent to which many receptions are engaged with, at best, a fuzzy, non-academic and partly imaginary version of what we see as the Real Thing. A proper study of classical reception in, say, eighteenth-century American political thought or twentieth-century classical music may primarily involve an analysis of eighteenth-century American political thought or twentieth-century classical music, not classics, requiring detailed knowledge of those contexts and traditions and the relevant scholarship. There are classical scholars who develop such expertise in these additional fields that their findings are equally persuasive to specialists – but this isn't universally true. Classicists need to take seriously the expertise of other disciplines, and the specificity of other historical contexts, either by doing the work to get up to speed or through proper collaboration; we need to recognize the validity of the research agendas of the other field, where the classical element may be just one strand in a broader investigation, rather than assuming that our questions are the important ones. Potentially, however, this is an enormously exciting area for future collaborative research, as the study of classical reception moves from its traditional base in literary and artistic studies, considering how creative artists have looked back to ancient texts and objects in their work, to explore classical influences in whole new areas of modern thought and culture.

The Politics of Reception

Classical reception, at any rate since Greek and Rome culture ceased to be taken for granted as the basis of all knowledge, is always political. This is clear enough when it involves explicitly political matters. It's impossible to separate changing modern views of Athenian democracy – from seeing it as a terrifying vision of the irrationality of the mob in the seventeenth century to offering it as a positive vision of popular engagement in the nineteenth – from the development of contemporary ideas about sovereignty, the relationship between state and people, and new models of citizenship. Neither discourse can be reduced to the other, but each is constantly influencing and responding to the other, and apparently innocuous historical statements about the statecraft of Pericles or the populist rhetoric of Cleon inevitably carried (carry?) a contemporary political charge. Similarly with Rome, whether through its influence (filtered through Polybius, and read alongside a range of other historical examples and theories) on the political institutions of the United States, or its role as the archetypal empire, a model for actual empires (especially in their self-image and visual identity), and a convenient disparaging comparison for other organizations that threaten the sacrosanct nation state, like the European Union or the United Nations.

The classical past may be, and often is, put into the service of the state, the monarch or the ruling elite – who do, after all, have command of the necessary knowledge (or scholars to digest it for them and present it in a suitable form) and the resources to put it into practice. The dependence of our knowledge of antiquity on the patronage of the wealthy is often underestimated; likewise numerous examples of classical reception, in art, literature, architecture and thought, owe their existence to the classicizing tastes of social elites. But knowledge of ancient culture and history can equally well serve a revolutionary purpose, as Karl Marx discussed in his essay 'The 18th Brumaire of Louis Bonaparte' (1851–2), looking back at the French Revolution:

> Unheroic as bourgeois society is, it nevertheless took heroism, sacrifice, terror, civil war and battles of peoples to bring it into being. And in the classically austere traditions of the Roman republic, its gladiators found the ideals and the art forms, the self-deceptions that they needed in order to conceal from themselves the bourgeois limitations of the content of their struggles and to keep their

enthusiasm on the high plane of the great historical tragedy. . . .[2]

Engagement with antiquity reveals that momentous historical change is possible, that things have not always been as they are now. The French Revolutionaries could dare to challenge the king because they knew that the Romans had overthrown their kings in the name of liberty, and had founded a glorious empire as a result. These ideas of the past may be idealized and simplified, sometimes to an absurd degree, but they have the power to open up new imaginative possibilities, to show that things could be different in the future because they have been different in the past.

The transformative potential of antiquity doesn't necessarily involve the overthrow of capitalism; classical precedent can support smaller but no less significant changes. An obvious example is the importance of ancient Greek culture in gay history, including the work of pioneering gay classicists like John Addington Symonds: classical culture as a respectable basis for admiring male beauty and talking about male friendship and attraction – Achilles and Patroclus, Alcibiades and Socrates – and the simple, gradually admitted historical fact that, for aristocratic Athenians, at least to judge from some of their writings, such relationships were an accepted part of social life. The modern scholarly argument that discussions of 'Greek homosexuality' may be misleading and anachronistic, that the Greeks conceived of such relationships quite differently, may be beside the point; this undoubtedly idealized idea of antiquity served its purpose in legitimizing the idea of homosexual relationships. Any discussion of ancient sexual mores is inevitably political, reflecting back on our own practices and revealing them to be purely customary and hence capable of being changed.

Even when it is not being used to reflect upon current political arrangements, or to criticize the current state of society, classical culture remains political, simply because it is received and reinterpreted within a network of political structures and relationships. There is always a struggle over its ownership, over who gets to claim and define it. Since the nineteenth century, classical knowledge has been wrested, at least partially, from the hands of the ruling classes, men and heterosexuals; we no longer see the past solely through their eyes, preconceptions and preferences, and no longer allow them to deploy it in defence of their own status without criticism. But we have barely begun the struggle to free classical antiquity from the claim that it is the exclusive inheritance of one self-identified 'race'. From an early stage, the Greeks and Romans were identified as white, as the ancestors of modern Europeans and their descendants across the globe – even if this involved denying that heritage to the present-day inhabitants of Greece on the grounds of their racial inferiority. The possession of this cultural legacy, assumed without question to be superior to anything that decadent Asiatics or primitive Africans could offer, legitimized conquest and slavery. Evidence that the glories of Greece and the grandeur of Rome might have owed anything to other, inferior civilizations was ignored or quietly passed over; classical figures were depicted as white Europeans, without any hint of the hybridity and cultural exchange that characterized the Mediterranean world in reality.

The claim that classical culture is the root of 'Our Civilization', and that the Greeks and Romans are us as we are them – 'Even our culture's ruins look amazing!', tweeted an American woman alongside a picture of an ancient theatre in Turkey – becomes a claim to exclusive ownership. The classics of the classical canon are incorporated into Great Books courses as the original Dead White European Males (male and dead, yes, but the other two labels beg the question), denying space to texts from a wider range of cultures with the implication that this is entirely right and proper because they are simply superior – and so are we, their white heirs. Texts and objects which could be treated as part of the common heritage of humanity are interpreted in terms of an intrinsic whiteness which other cultural traditions will inevitably fail to understand or appreciate – a failure which is then taken as a mark of their inferiority. If classics does not recognize how far it has been and still is implicated in such processes of exclusion and myth-making, then it will come to matter in the contemporary world in precisely the wrong way – as a weapon in the hands of cultural conservatives, and an object of mistrust and derision to everyone else.

Reinventing Antiquity

There is, as we have seen, no single, stable antiquity, but rather a multitude of worlds, a kaleidoscope of possible examples and influences, different sorts of objects and texts, that can be viewed from many different perspectives. Likewise, ancient texts and objects can always be interpreted in multiple ways; some more plausible or at least more widely accepted than others, but always open to challenge and revision. It is scarcely surprising, therefore, that antiquity has also been received by later ages in innumerable, often inconsistent and regularly contradictory ways. In the moment of reception, antiquity is always to some extent (sometimes to a great extent) reinvented – even if the receiver honestly believes that he or she is being as faithful to the original as possible. 'Meaning is realized at the point of reception' is a cliché of this area of research, emphasizing not only the unmistakable fact that this happens, time and again, but also that the role of the scholar is to understand and interpret the reinvention, *not* to judge it against a supposedly authentic and/or superior original.

In other words, the historical accuracy of Shakespeare's *Julius Caesar* – anachronistic striking clocks and all – is beside the point. We're not even concerned with how far he rewrites Plutarch's already-distorted account of the man's life; or, rather, the relationship between different sources, and how and why things get modified, is an important strand of research, but it isn't a yardstick by which to judge Shakespeare's achievement. What matters is how Shakespeare (re)invents Caesar and his final days for his own purposes, drawing on ancient material and making something new out of it. As with any text, let alone a complex work of art, we can read it in many different ways: the play sheds light on contemporary knowledge of ancient history and how this was valued; it reveals how ancient models might be employed to comment surreptitiously on current events or on pressing political problems; it establishes a dialogue between different perspectives on past and present. It emphasizes the power and potential of the classical to be reused and reimagined, not its power to limit what posterity might make of it.

In a similar manner, the East German writer Christa Wolf looked back in her novel *Cassandra* (1983) to Homer's *Iliad* and Aeschylus' *Agamemnon*, both as an oblique way to comment on her own society (Troy under siege becomes more and more a paranoid police state, seeking to silence Cassandra for telling the truth about the reality of the situation) and as a means of engaging with wider issues about war and the way that women are too often its victims but endure this silently.

> In the citadel there seemed to be only one single man who knew the answer to the shameful exuberance of the enemy; the man was Eumelos. He turned the screws. He threw his security net, which previously had suffocated the members of the royal house and the officials, over the whole of Troy; it now affected everyone. The citadel completely

sealed after nightfall. Strict controls on what one can carry, whenever Eumelos considers something is forbidden. Special powers for the relevant agents.

Eumelos, I said, this is impossible. (Of course I knew that it was possible). And why? he asked with icy politeness. Because this way we will harm ourselves more than the Greeks. I would gladly hear more from you about that, he said. At that moment fear gripped me. Eumelos, I called, pleadingly, something about which I still feel ashamed: Believe me! I want the same thing as you do.

He pressed his lips hard together. I couldn't win him over. He said formally: Excellent. So you will support our measures.[3]

The Trojan legend works as a basis for this exploration because it is so familiar, and therefore the reader can appreciate the ways in which Wolf's retelling of the story through the eyes of Cassandra – and the juxtaposition of the languages of epic and the Stasi – offers a different perspective on events. It's the same reason why retellings of the Odyssey or Greek myth never go out of fashion: the artist can explore the elasticity and flexibility of the original, draw on its cultural prestige, and play on its existing associations; the audience can appreciate both the familiarity and the variation. And, by revealing its potential for meaning something new in the present, the original also appears in a new light: Wolf also draws out the inherent cruelty and violence of Homer's poem, its glorification of masculine aggression and destructiveness, which continues to legitimize it in the present. Receiving the *Iliad*, Wolf reflects on its past reception and influence, and makes us read it differently in the future.

The resourcefulness of modern artists and thinkers in their reinventions of antiquity, and the capacity of antiquity to be reinvented, are causes for celebration. But the malleability of antiquity can also be a cause for concern, when we view the many ways in which classical culture has been turned to uses which make us uncomfortable. Can we object to certain reinventions, and start using the language of 'appropriation' and 'misinterpretation', on the basis that we don't like the results? It isn't hard to think of examples: the wholesale use of classical symbolism, architecture and sculpture by twentieth-century totalitarian regimes; the citation of Aristotle and other classical sources to legitimize chattel slavery; the adoption of Spartan symbolism in the memes and regalia of the alt-right and European far-right movements; the film *300* (2006), about which the least said the better. Insofar as these claim some sort of historical legitimacy, that they are true representations of the past, we can offer refutations (however unproductive). But the fact that *our* idea of the classical isn't like this doesn't give us grounds suddenly for claiming that playful, present-focused reinvention is allowed only for people like us. Rather, we need to acknowledge that classical culture is unavoidably open to such uses, like any other knowledge, and is likely to be deployed in this way precisely because of its continuing power and resonance. We can and should object on political and moral grounds; but we can't sudden start yelling about authenticity, when we know that there is no basis for such a claim.

It is more important, if painful, for classicists to face up to the fact that some of our beloved ancient culture is not only open to such uses but positively welcomes them. The Nazi cult of strength, beauty and purity was partly the end result of a centuries-long tradition of idealizing Greece in such terms – but it has unmistakable roots in the Greeks' own worship of strength and power. The ancient world was dominated by aristocratic warrior cultures, glorifying war and inequality; the Spartans were simply the best organized, most militarized and least cultured of a deeply unpleasant bunch. Just as a slave always rode in the chariot of a triumphant Roman general, whispering in his ear that he is still mortal, so we need our own invisible voice, constantly reminding us that behind every Roman general, behind every achievement of classical culture, there lie the beaten and exhausted bodies of countless slaves. This doesn't mean that we should feel permanently guilty about our aesthetic response to classical art and literature, or wholly mistrust our instinctive sense of familiarity and comradeship with certain writers, but we do need to recognize how far these responses are conditioned by centuries of the classical tradition, and how far we are still tempted to skim over the less comfortable aspects of the ancient world.

Understanding the present, and the multiple traces of Greece and Rome that persist in it, needs classicists to help understand and interpret the ways in which antiquity has been received and reinvented; but all classicists, even those focused solely on antiquity rather than its later echoes, need to pay attention to the history of reception and its impact on their understanding. The classical past is never a refuge from the present; it always bears its mark.

4

Anticipating the Future?

Useful Knowledge

We can study the past as an end in itself, and as a means of understanding important aspects of the present; we don't have to argue that the classical world has some special, intrinsic value or significance to recognize that it has had an important influence – if only because people in previous generations *thought* that the classical world, or at least certain aspects of it, had some special, intrinsic value and status within the western tradition. This is one argument for why classics continues to matter; but it's an open question whether it's enough to silence the critics of the humanities, arguing that these disciplines are unaffordable luxuries in a world which desperately needs the work of scientists and engineers to save us from impending global catastrophe and/or ensure the continuing performance of our economy (delete according to ideological preference). There is the undeniable beauty, power and fascination of much classical writing and art, but that butters no parsnips. We can of course put forward a case for the numerous transferable skills that studying classics develops: the ability to research, analyse, interpret, cope with uncertainty and ambiguity, and present all this in neatly argued forms in multiple formats. As an academic subject, classics may not equip students for a specific profession, but it doesn't rule out anything that hasn't already been excluded by a decision not to pursue STEM subjects in the first place. Arguably, an ever more uncertain future, not least the threatened rise of automation, calls for precisely these sorts of general analytical abilities, and a flexibility of outlook, rather than skills that are geared to jobs that may be handed over to robots and AI within a decade. The obvious problem with this case is that such skills can equally well be developed in other humanities and social science disciplines, arguably with a greater relevance to the contemporary world; and, even if classics can show that it's no more of a decorative indulgence than other humanities subjects, it could be argued that it needs to justify itself *more* than they do, to compensate for its long tradition of supporting dubious political agendas and social division . . .

Is there a stronger case to be made for the usefulness of studying classical antiquity? At the least, ancient Greece offers us the first concerted attempts at making that sort of argument, when Thucydides sought to persuade his readers that they would learn more from him than mere facts:

> Perhaps the absence of the element of fable in my work may make it seem less easy on the ear; but it will have served its purpose well enough if it is judged useful by those who want to have a clear view of what happened in the past and what – the human condition being what it is – can be expected to happen again some time in the future in similar or much the same ways. It is composed to be a possession for all time and not just a performance-piece for the moment.[1]

Thucydides deliberately challenges his potential readers: you shouldn't try to read this work if you're just looking for entertainment or the confirmation of your existing views, and reading it won't necessarily be a pleasurable experience, but *you*, dear reader, one of the chosen few, will recognize its unique qualities and come to feel superior to all those who fail to appreciate this. You will not only gain a true, reliable knowledge of what happened in the past; this will also help you understand the present and the future.

There is a long tradition of reading Thucydides in exactly these terms. Historians of all periods have extended his claim to historiography in general – 'those who forget the past are condemned to repeat it', as the American philosopher George Santayana argued – and offered it as a justification for their entire enterprise, without necessarily explaining *how* knowledge of the past will be useful. More concretely, as noted above, Thucydides has been interpreted instead as a pioneer in political science and international relations theory, as someone who took the raw data of events as the basis for developing general theories about politics and inter-state relations which can then be used to predict future developments. For the last few years, almost any discussion of relations between the United States and China has tended to mention the Thucydides Trap, a theory in which Thucydides' statement about the origins of the Peloponnesian War – 'it was the growth of Athens, and the fear this aroused in Sparta, that made war unavoidable' – is understood as a trans-historical principle, which now implies that tensions between an established America and a rising China could lead to conflict much more easily than most people think. 'Exiled Thucydides knew,' as W. H. Auden remarked of the outbreak of the Second World War, and numerous readers have identified the way that the insights of his account seem to remain relevant.[2]

Granted, these interpretations of Thucydides as social scientist tend to ignore the detailed philological investigations of the classicists, who might insist on arguing about whether this is really what Thucydides meant – it's a warning sign that the continued importance of classical authorities for present-day discussions doesn't necessarily require classicists. Still, we could take this as an indication of the potential for bringing ancient knowledge into the present, if only because of the continuing authority that's ascribed to classical culture. We might then consider what other ancient authors could be brought forward to offer similar insights: the philosophers, certainly, with their general theories of human society, but also other historians. In fact the idea of a 'Tacitus Trap' – that there is a tipping point after which rulers and governments lose all credibility with the public whatever they do – has already been developed in China.

Any such attempt at learning from the past rests on the assumption of some kind of underlying continuity; we need to have grounds for assuming that events and situations might resemble one another to a sufficient degree that we can safely develop predictions about the future on the basis of the past. Thucydides is understood to have set out to uncover such regularities, and to have identified them in a constant 'human nature' or 'the human condition', so that we can identify through his work consistent tendencies in the behaviour of states (governed by the three forces of fear, interest and honour), in the nature of the international system ('the strong do what they can and the weak endure what they must', as in the famous Melian Dialogue) and the origins of conflict. Of course, it so happens that these principles are ones which were already held by Realist thinkers in international relations, who now discover them in the past and claim classical authority for their views . . .

When we humanists study the past, however, we tend to emphasize difference and specificity, the ways in which different historical contexts vary in numerous ways; we are sceptical of claims about trans-historical principles and continuities, precisely because our detailed study of the past tends to put them in question. For the purposes of trying to draw lessons from the past, and of persuading non-classicists that we have useful lessons to offer, this is clearly an inconvenience, but we would not be true to our discipline if we denied it. We see clearly that Thucydides offers only one interpretation of the past, not its objective reality, and that other interpretations are always possible. The past is not an objective body of data against which modern theories can be measured, but an infinite storehouse of possible analogies and examples, depending on what we're looking for – and those who look back to it do tend to find what they're looking for. We classicists can certainly try to rein back our constant obsession with difference and our hostility to generalization, but only so far, before the past is simply reduced to a pale copy of the present that is then offered as proof of the absolute superiority of present understanding. Yes, Thucydides can be read as a kind of social scientist, but we classicists do have to point out that most of the principles attributed to him were actually put into the mouths of characters in his account, and can't simply be taken as his own views. The prominence of Thucydides in modern debates, even to the point of being discussed in the White House, is another example of reception, rather than a solid basis for claiming that classics is actually useful. The fact that Thucydides is currently in fashion, and that our times do appear rather Thucydidean, might be taken as a sign to run to the hills instead or to start digging a bunker; but mostly these are grounds for expressing scepticism about drawing universal principles from the past, and about the reasons why anyone would invoke classical authority to support them.

It's the End of the World as We Know It . . .

Edward Gibbon closed his magisterial *History of the Decline and Fall of the Roman Empire* in 1776 with a complex meditation on change and decay: he introduces us to a fifteenth-century humanist scholar called Poggius and a friend, who climbed the Capitoline Hill one day and gazed over the city of Rome.

> The place and the object gave ample scope for moralising on the vicissitudes of fortune, which spares neither man nor the proudest of his works, which buries empires and cities in a common grave; and it was agreed that in proportion to her former greatness the fall of Rome was the more awful and deplorable.

Consider the contrast between then and now, remarks Poggius.

> The hill of the Capitol, on which we sit, was formerly the head of the Roman empire, the citadel of the earth, the terror of kings; illustrated by the

footsteps of so many triumphs, enriched with the spoils and tributes of so many nations. This spectacle of the world, how is it fallen! how changed! how defaced! The path of victory is obliterated by vines, and the benches of the senators are concealed by a dunghill.

So much for worldly power and the glories of classical civilization! Gibbon proceeds to summarize his views on the causes of the depredations of Rome's great monuments, namely 'I. The injuries of time and nature', 'II. The hostile attacks of the Barbarians and Christians', 'III. The use and abuse of the materials' and 'IV. The domestic quarrels of the Romans'[3] – with particular emphasis on the latter – and observes that it was the contemplation of the ruins of the Capitol that led him to embark on his history: the greatest, perhaps, and most awful scene in the history of mankind.

The remnants of classical antiquity regularly offer an occasion for imagining the future of our own society; all things come to pass, and so too the present, however great and permanent it may appear. As the comte de Volney said to himself in 1784 when studying classical ruins:

Who knows, said I, but such may one day be the abandonment of our own countries? Who knows

108

if on the banks of the Seine, the Thames, or the Zuyder-zee, where now, in the vortex of so many enjoyments, the heart and the eye suffice not for the multitude of sensations, who knows if some traveller, like me, shall not one day sit on their silent ruins, and weep in solitude over the ashes of their people, and the memory of their greatness?[4]

It seems to be a short step from such pleasurable reflections to wondering whether ancient history might tell us more about the decline and fall of modern civilization than the simple idea that it will not last for ever. We might look to the past not for underlying continuities and universal principles, but for a sense of the rhythms of change and the dynamics of development. If history is cyclical, with different societies passing through the same stages of growth, maturity and decline, then we can identify our own position in the cycle and thus predict our future.

Rome offers the most useful examples, or certainly the most commonly used, above all because the Romans – at least to judge from the surviving sources – seem to have felt themselves to be permanently in decline, sadly inferior to their glorious ancestors. The idea, developed by the historian Sallust, that the Roman Republic fell because it was corrupted by wealth and luxury became a recurrent theme in political debates in the seventeenth and eighteenth centuries – until writers like Adam Smith managed to convince his readers that material prosperity, even for ordinary people, might be morally neutral. Republican concerns about the decay of civic spirit and the rise of a populist autocrat, bringing an end to liberty, found echoes in the mid-twentieth century and have resurfaced in recent years with the triumphs of figures like Putin, Erdoğan and Trump. The claims of Augustan propaganda about the decadence of the later republic, characterized by the excessive freedom of women and the decline of the traditional family, the decline of religion, unemployment and excessive consumption, have been taken up by the Belgian ancient historian David Engels to demonstrate that Europe may be on the verge of civil war, to be succeeded in twenty or thirty years' time by the rise of a new popularly acclaimed dictator.[5]

But above all it's the great narrative of Decline and Fall that is most commonly believed to hold the key to our own fate. One problem for would-be soothsayers is that there are multiple explanations of this phenomenon, and the chosen story has changed dramatically over time. Edward Gibbon looked to religion and barbarism as the prime culprits, quietly insisting on his own Enlightenment values as the best hope for the future. French and Italian propaganda

Figure 3: Italian First World War propaganda poster: the goddess Italia confronts an invading barbarian. (Getty Images)

against Germany and Austria in the First World War regularly evoked the image of savage barbarians threatening Civilization (Figure 3). The great ancient historian Michael Rostovtzeff, in exile from revolutionary Russia, located the essence of classical civilization in the educated middle classes of the cities, and worried both that (as had happened in

Rome) modern civilization was doomed unless it could be extended to the rural masses, and that such a civilization would inevitably become debased as a result of being disseminated. Another important name in ancient history in the first half of the twentieth century, the American Tenney Frank, wrote about the destructive effects of 'race mixture' in Roman society, drawing explicit and uncritical parallels with contemporary fears of miscegenation and the alien within. Modern agitators offer similar arguments about immigrants and their alien customs diluting or swamping 'pure' European culture, or indeed seizing power themselves through violence, as well as denouncing the decadence of western societies that leads them to deny the threat and fail to defend against it. They offer themselves as the true defenders of 'Western Civilization', not least by adopting classical imagery – albeit sometimes in unusual forms (Figure 4).

Practical advice, rather than all-purpose doom-saying and overt racism, is in shorter supply, beyond a call to defend the borders in the way that the Romans supposedly failed to do. The American author Morris Berman, fearing the debasement of western culture in the face of inequality, falling levels of literacy, cynicism, apathy, political corruption and cultural decay, proposed the establishment

Figure 4: An example of contemporary 'fashwave' alt-right imagery. Classical virtue for a future fascist society?

of monastery-like establishments where true knowledge could be preserved and the beleaguered elites could shelter from the new Dark Ages – though, after 9/11, like many others, his attention switched to the 'barbarians at the gates'.[6] For the most part, contemporary comparisons are offered above all as camouflage for anti-foreigner and anti-Islamic rhetoric: 'We're not prejudiced. They are a threat to our entire civilization! Remember Rome!' Many of these comparisons are trite, if not downright silly; piling up disconnected examples and presenting them in a way that emphazises possible resemblances (for example: just as the invading barbarians used Rome's excellent network of roads, so the terrorists of September 11 used America's aviation schools, banking systems and internet). The many differences between past and present are ignored, for obvious reasons. It scarcely needs to be said that more detailed, specialist studies of the crisis of the Roman Empire do not lead to better, more detailed predictions about current and future developments, but to a questioning of the utility of these comparisons at all.

What can and should we do with these apocalyptic visions? We can see how the Romans told stories about their own past as a means of commenting on the present, and how their actions in the present were shaped by ideas about the past. We can certainly explore these modern narratives of decline and fall in similar terms, comparing them both with Roman precedents and with the interpretations offered by later centuries: the way, for example, that such accounts serve a psychological need – people would apparently rather *know* that they are doomed, 'because History', than deal with uncertainty. It is striking also how these narratives emphasize certain sorts of threat above others. The substantial evidence suggesting that climate change and environmental degradation played a role in the crises of the later Roman Empire, not least by triggering the mass movement of peoples across Eurasia, has not been widely used to support calls for urgent action to tackle modern climate change. Instead, evidence of historical environmental conditions (including the so-called 'Roman Warm Period') is more likely to be mustered to try to demonstrate that changes in global temperature are completely natural and shouldn't be any cause for concern. Accounts of violent hordes streaming across the border, however, are ten a penny, deployed to mobilize support for more repressive policies towards migrants on the grounds that we *know* from history what the consequences of inaction and tolerance will be.

The primary role of classical studies is not to indulge such accounts but to question them – to return to the facts, to re-emphasize the complexity of the world and the uncertainty of our knowledge of the past. That latter point is, of course, a problem – the caution of academics, refusing to go beyond what the evidence will support, will always appear to offer a weaker story than those offered by the polemicists and far-right agitators. But we're never going to persuade such people, as they are not concerned with historical arguments in good faith; our audience has to be those without such ideological commitments, who might be swayed by confident assertions about the lessons of the past but who might still listen to those with some claim to expertise in the subject.

The Human Thing

What Thucydides really offers in his work – what he meant by 'the human condition' – is a sense of the many ways in which people are terrible judges of their own situation and very bad at decision-making, prone to both excessive optimism and excessive pessimism, to exuberance and panic, and highly susceptible to manipulative rhetoric. In other words, he actually cautions against any attempt at reducing a complex, unpredictable world to simple rules and principles – let alone basing our decisions on confident predictions about what will happen, 'because History'. Thucydides emphasizes the limits of our knowledge, the degree of uncertainty inherent in any situation; the fact that things could well have turned out differently. The eternal cry of the humanities scholar, that 'actually it's all much more complicated than that', based on our extensive study of how the past has indeed been complex and unpredictable, is not so much a problem, preventing us from offering useful guidance to the present, as our essential contribution to the discussion.

Anticipating the Future?

It's sometimes observed that classicists are consumers rather than producers of theory; magpie-like, we gather ideas from every other discipline that seems to offer something useful for our purposes, but fail to do anything with them that might be useful to anyone else. There is an alternative way of looking at this: we take the confident claims of other disciplines to explain the world, or at least aspects of it, and stress test them to destruction. We confront would-be universal principles with the fact that human societies differ greatly from one another; we put theories developed to explain one carefully delineated sector of modern society into the Colosseum of competing theories, breaking down the artificial boundaries between, say, economy, society, culture and politics. We offer constant reminders of the fact that the world *is* complex and multi-faceted; that human beings – including figures like Plato, not just modern social scientists – can offer powerful insights into its workings by isolating certain aspects and deliberately ignoring complexity for the sake of analysis, but that such insights are only ever partial and limited, and can be dangerously misleading if one then assumes that the world ought to conform to them.

The study of classical antiquity, like the study of any other society, expands our knowledge and understanding of the human, the ways in which our species may be both predictable and unpredictable. We can identify certain tendencies in the past, the ways that humans do often respond in similar ways to certain situations and the recurrence of similar problems in different contexts; but also the ways in which they may respond quite differently to apparently similar situations, and the reasons behind this. The experiences of past humans cannot tell us with confidence what humans in the present or future will do; but they offer a corrective to overly confident claims from other disciplines about what humans will do. This may work as a kind of precautionary principle, guarding against simplistic assumptions. We know that, in many important respects, the present is different from the past (let alone the classical past) and that therefore this time things may be different; but we can also draw on past experience to open up our sense of the possibilities. We can guard against the triumphalism of the present, since it is clear that ancient societies were highly complex and sophisticated in their own ways; but we can also guard against the temptation to tell stories of past greatness and present decline, to idealize the lost past. Above all, studying classical antiquity, and especially the works of some of its most acute commentators, emphasizes the importance of perspective and the role of cultural filters and assumptions in shaping decisions. Reading Homer, or Thucydides, or Plato, or Cicero, or any other ancient text, doesn't offer answers; but it points to the need to ask questions and acknowledge uncertainty.

This kind of perspective greatly expands the range of texts and examples that may usefully be brought into dialogue with the present and its possible futures: not just those that look more or less like modern social science, offering clear predictions or principles of social and political organization, but anything that tells us what it is to be human; not a single unchanging human type, let along an idealized human or superhuman, but the whole range of strength, weakness, creativity and conflict. Greek tragedy does this to a superlative degree, but so too do the characters of Homer and Virgil, the speculations of Plato, Aristotle, Seneca and Augustine, the events described by the historians – and the records of more ordinary lives, preserved in inscriptions and graffiti and the simple objects of everyday existence.

Futures Past

Classics does not offer predictions or forecasts about the future, but its potential contribution is not limited to the role of Cassandra, warning – perhaps fruitlessly – against the risks of over-confidence and arrogance. Thinking productively about the future is not just about trying to predict it – indeed, there's a case to be made, not least from past experience, that attempting to predict anything about future developments is a fruitless exercise – but also about considering what kind of future we actually want. If our destination is not already written, then we have the power, collectively, to strive to reach one place rather than another. The past shows us that other ways of life have been possible, and so could be again – if we choose them.

This does not imply a revival of the old tradition of idealizing the classical world as a counterpoint to the debasement and degradation of modernity; this sort of speculation, if it is to be productive, depends on us having a clear idea of the limitations of ancient practices as well as their attractive features. Antiquity is not a model, in the sense of something we should slavishly copy, but we can identify certain aspects that represent things we would want to re-create in the future – and we can use our knowledge of antiquity to think this through more carefully. An obvious example is democracy. We use the same label for our political systems as the Athenians did, although the differences are numerous and obvious. There is a polemical tradition of contrasting the two, implying that our system is not a *real* democracy – and wouldn't it be great if we still had the Athenian custom of ostracism, sending polarizing political figures into temporary banishment by popular vote? (I will confess to finding this idea rather attractive at times.) But there is a more productive tradition of trying to understand the differences and their underlying causes. Is a representative democracy simply a practical solution to giving the mass of the population a political role, despite the fact that we now live in political communities of millions of people rather than the tiny face-to-face society of the Greek *polis*? If technology now makes the idea of a return to direct popular voting on every issue at least theoretically possible, is this something we should actively work towards – given what we can see of its consequences in Athens, and the various critiques offered by contemporary authors like Plato, Thucydides and Aristophanes? Did Athenian participatory democracy depend on slave labour, as is sometimes argued – and, if it did, is this something we can now overcome? Is the image of a culturally homogeneous community of patriots, as depicted in Pericles' Funeral Oration, the goal we should be striving for, or a nightmare of conformity and rhetorical manipulation?

Anticipating the Future?

Thinking about the future is not just a matter of imagining goals and possible destinations; the past also offers us images of nightmares so that we know what we want to avoid. The most powerful passages in Thucydides are those which depict the breakdown of social ties and cultural norms; a constant theme in all areas of classical literature is the abuse of power by tyrants and self-centred elites. The extent to which ancient society rested on the exploitation and degradation of human beings, above all slaves but also women and the mass of the population, is not just a cause for modern self-satisfaction about our progress; it is a warning against a return to that sort of society, simply because no one recognized the signs or thought to try to stop it. We do have to consider the possibility of futures that we would not want to live in (see, for example, the ideas put forward in Peter Frase's *Four Futures*); antiquity offers a broad repertoire of appalling possibilities as a basis for such speculation.

This is an eminently classical enterprise; ancient literature is full of attempts at imagining different worlds, as a means of commenting on the present and trying to shape possible futures. Lucian depicted a journey to the moon; Aristophanes imagined all sorts of fantastic scenarios – an Athens in which women ruled or a world in which poverty was abolished – partly as a source of laughs but above all in order to explore the implications and consequences of such a transformation of present conditions. Plato developed a utopia, the imaginary city of the *Republic*, as a means of thinking through questions about justice or the nature of community to their logical conclusion. The *Republic* has a claim to be the earliest example of one brand of speculative science fiction, an idea that's developed in the Thessaly novels of Jo Walton, depicting the establishment of a real version of Plato's city as a means both of commenting on his vision and of exploring further questions of what a truly good political community might look like. And this is another way in which engagement with classical antiquity can aid our attempts at imagining possible futures and preparing for them: classics offers not only material, but also new ideas about forms and methods; thinking about the world not only through analytical treatises and abstract theories but also through drama, comedy, art, performance. It expands our resources and our possibilities; it offers us a vantage point on our times and assumptions; it is part of our inheritance as human beings, and yet it forces us to question everything about what it is to be human, and to be us. Let me leave the final word to Friedrich Nietzsche:

For I do not know what meaning classical studies would have in our time, if not that of working in their untimeliness – that is to say, against our time and thereby on our time and, let us hope, for the benefit of a time to come.[7]

Afterword

One of the incidental pleasures of writing this book has been imagining the likely reactions of certain friends, distinguished colleagues and media commentators on classical subjects to the fact that I of all people was writing it. Isn't Morley an ancient historian, rather than a proper classicist? Indeed, has he not on occasion been quite insulting about the deficiencies of traditional classics when it comes to studying the history of the ancient world? And this is before they actually read what I've written about their beloved discipline. Couldn't Polity have got a proper classicist to write this alleged defence and justification of the subject?

It's certainly true that my main focus over twenty-odd years as a professional teacher and researcher on classical antiquity has been on 'historical' subjects, broadly defined – I've certainly never worked on philological issues or written a commentary on a text, and my ability to appreciate Latin poetry (let alone compose it) or spot subtle intertextual references is, to say the least, negligible. I have sometimes in the past characterized myself as 'a historian who does ancient stuff', for fear of becoming too distanced from mainstream historical research and too closely associated with the sort of ancient history that focuses solely and uncritically on ancient elites and their preoccupations. I do have some command of Greek and Latin, sufficient for the purposes of my research, but – as you will probably have gathered – I am deeply suspicious of the claim that *only* those with high-level abilities in ancient languages can aspire to study the classical world seriously, and so am quite happy to be denied the title of being a Proper Classicist. In many respects, I find the tradition of classical studies, and the ways in which people have used classical antiquity for different purposes, very troubling.

And yet I am deeply committed to the study of classical antiquity and its legacy; I may never be a proper classicist, or comfortable about being called one, but if there was a convenient English translation of the German *Altertumswissenschaftler*, encompassing all the different aspects of the subject rather than just the historical, I would happily adopt it. 'Classical studies' is not, in my view, a defective or inferior version of classics for the linguistically challenged, as it's sometimes regarded by traditionalists; it stands for the sort of comprehensive, comparative and multi-disciplinary approach to the study of antiquity that fits the way that my teaching and research have developed since I was a snotty and rather more narrow-minded graduate student, arguing with Mary Beard about whether 'classicist' was an identity to be proud of.

I would not now be so dogmatic, which is one reason why, after some hesitation, I was delighted to accept the invitation to write this book. In part, this is simply because over the last couple of decades my interests have developed and expanded, to encompass less narrowly historical themes like classical reception (in literature as well as in sober social-scientific and philosophical discussions), cultural and intellectual history, and above all the endless complexities of Thucydides, so that I spend more time these days engaging with research on literary and philosophical themes than I used to. In part, it is because classical studies itself has changed and continues to change, so that – at least in some contexts – the divisions, ideological differences and turf wars between different approaches that I remember from my student days have become less significant or meaningful. Not only can we have productive conversations with one another, it's increasingly clear that *only* through such conversations can we really advance our knowledge and understanding of the most important questions about ancient societies and cultures. Today's classical studies is a vibrant, innovative, sophisticated and thoughtful field of study; why would I not want to be a part of that?

The third aspect of this intellectual journey has been a growing sense of the need to defend the whole tradition of classical studies – not only the historical realities of the classical past, but the multiple strands of its influence, tradition and reinterpretation – against external threats. Some of these threats are obvious and familiar: the ongoing tendency to downgrade humanistic subjects, or at least to force them to conform to narrow instrumentalist priorities, in schools and universities – and, indeed, the evident annoyance of some figures in government and other positions of authority that students persist in wanting to study such subjects. We classicists are all too used to marginalization, disparagement and imminent financial catastrophe, and it is certainly worth reiterating what I think are the real contributions that studying this discipline can make to our world's future, including questioning the priorities of some of those who seek to dictate that future. But classical studies – more than many other humanities disciplines – is also threatened by people who claim to value it, but who then seek to confine it within a limited and traditional conception of Proper Classics, or to limit access to it to a privileged elite, or to deploy the cultures of classical antiquity in support of their ideological agendas.

This final point has become ever more obvious while I was writing this book – and the book has become angrier and more explicitly political as a result. Classical antiquity has been more visible in the wider public discourse in the last few years, I suspect, than it has been for decades, if not a century, but not always in ways with which professional students of the period will feel wholly comfortable. The ancient world and its legacy have become explicitly politicized, whether we like it or not: it *matters* to certain people whether Roman Britain was a multi-ethnic society, or whether classical statues were painted rather than left as white marble, or whether the Roman Empire was overwhelmed by waves of migrants or hostile barbarians, or whether Thucydides demonstrates the inevitable triumph of power over justice. These debates may often have little to do with the realities of classical antiquity, insofar as we can recover that, or with current scholarly understanding – indeed, what was surprising about the 2017 arguments on social media about whether there were people of African origin in Britain or whether white marble statues are anachronistic is that these are things that were firmly established within the scholarly community years ago – but that doesn't let us off the hook. We are faced with a choice, between trying to combat such myths and misconceptions – with the problem that our careful qualifications about what we can and can't know, given the state of the evidence, will always seem like pedantry and evasiveness to the alt-right keyboard warriors and assertive purveyors of pop social science – and allowing such misrepresentations to pass unchallenged in the world beyond the classroom, for the sake of a quieter life, while the more courageous and outspoken of our colleagues are deluged with misogynistic and anti-Semitic abuse and death threats for pushing back against such appropriations.

The task of classical studies is to understand classical antiquity and its legacy better, in all their different facets. But that is not only an end in itself; it is important because classical antiquity and its legacy still have power in our world, for good and ill. Whatever my classical colleagues may think about my version of classics as a discipline and why it matters, I hope they will share my view that it's worth arguing about, that classicists need to think about their place in the world and to engage with the world.

I am enormously grateful to Pascal Porcheron at Polity for the opportunity to write this book, to the anonymous reviewers for their comments and suggestions, and to Justin Dyer for his careful and sympathetic copy-editing. I should like to dedicate it to all the classicists who have inspired me in recent years, whether by illuminating classical antiquity and its legacy in new ways, by offering examples of intellectual and political engagement, or simply by forcing me to think about my own ideas more carefully and critically; among them Danielle Allen, Sarah Bond, Liz Gloyn, Emily Greenwood, Johanna Hanink, Katherine Harloe, Laura Jansen, Donna Zuckerberg and, as ever, Anne.

Notes

Chapter 1 What's Wrong with Classics

1 Friedrich Schiller, 'Die Götter Griechenlands' [1788], lines 17–20, in *Gedichte 1776–1799: Schillers Werke Nationalausgabe*, Vol. I, ed. J. Petersen & F. Beissner (Weimar, 1943), p. 190. My translation.

2 Karl Marx, *Grundrisse* [1857–8], trans. Martin Nicolaus (Harmondsworth, 1973).

3 Kate Tempest, *Brand New Ancients* (London, 2013), pp. 3–4.

4 James Joyce, *Ulysses*, episode 12, known as 'Cyclops' (Paris, 1922), p. 286.

5 John Keats, 'On First Looking into Chapman's Homer' [1816], in *The Complete Poems* (Harmondsworth, 1973), p. 72.

6 G.W.F. Hegel, 'On Classical Studies' [1809], trans. Richard Kroner, in *Early Theological Writings* (Philadelphia, 1975), p. 324.

7 Ibid., pp. 324–5.

8 *Down With Skool!* [1953], in Geoffrey Willans

& Ronald Searle, *Molesworth* (Harmondsworth, 1999), p. 39.

9 Friedrich Nietzsche, 'Wir Philologen' [1875], in *Werke*, Vol. 4.1 (Berlin, 1967). Translation of parts of the essay at https://archive.org/stream/wephilolo gists18267gut/18267.txt.

10 George Eliot, *Middlemarch* [1871–2] (Oxford, 1998), pp. 16–17.

11 Ibid., p. 17.

12 W.B. Yeats, 'The Scholars' [1914/15], in *Collected Poems* (London, 1950), p. 158.

13 Wilfred Owen, 'Dulce et Decorum est' [1917], in *Poems* (London, 1921), p. 15.

14 Derek Walcott, *Omeros*, Chapter XL.1.i (London, 1990), p. 206.

15 James Hilton, *Goodbye, Mr Chips* (London, 1934), pp. 19–20.

16 The contemporary examples cited here are, respectively: Boris Johnson: see, for instance, Charlotte Higgins, 'A Classic Toff', *Guardian*, 6 June 2008 (https://www.theguardian.com/commentisfree/2008/jun/06/classics.boris); Jacob Rees-Mogg (@Jacob_Rees_Mogg): https://twitter.com/Jacob_Rees_Mogg/status/886208542667046912; James Delingpole, 'For a Real Oxbridge Education, You Now Have to Go to Durham', *The Spectator*, 25 March 2017 (https://www.spectator.co.uk/2017/03/for-a-real-ox bridge-education-you-now-have-to-go-to-durham/).

17 Donna Tartt, *The Secret History* (Harmondsworth, 1992), p. 34.

18 Ibid., p. 604.

19 Tony Harrison, 'Classics Society' [1978], in *Selected Poems*, 2nd edn (Harmondsworth, 1987), p. 120.
20 Louis Stuart, 'Men Must be Educated in the Classics if They Wish to Regain Masculine Fortitude', Return of Kings.com, 8 July 2017 (http://www.returnof kings.com/125103/men-must-be-educated-in-the-classics-if-they-wish-to-regain-masculine-fortitude).

Chapter 2 Charting the Past

1 On the debate about the presence of 'Africans' in Roman Britain and the uses of genetic evidence, see articles by Caitlin Green ('A Note on the Evidence for African Migrants in Britain from the Bronze Age to the Medieval Period', 23 May 2016: http://www. caitlingreen.org/2016/05/a-note-on-evidence-for-af rican-migrants.html), Sarah Zhang ('A Kerfuffle About Diversity in the Roman Empire', *The Atlantic*, 2 August 2017: https://www.theatlantic. com/science/archive/2017/08/dna-romans/535701/) and Massimo Pigliucci ('Beard vs Taleb: Scientism and the Nature of Historical Inquiry', *iai news*, 11 August 2017: https://iainews.iai.tv/articles/beard-nassem-taleb-twitter-feud-and-dangers-of-scientism-auid-868?access=ALL).
2 On archaeology and the problem of a 'deserted' Italy, see Alessandro Launaro, *Peasants and Slaves: the rural population of Roman Italy* (Cambridge, 2011).
3 On the promotion of classical languages and classical studies in schools, see the websites of Advocating Classical Education (http://aceclassics.org.uk/) and

the Classical Association of the Middle West and South (https://camws.org/).

Chapter 3 Understanding the Present

1 On this and other aspects of the modern reception of Thucydides, see Neville Morley and Katherine Harloe, eds, *Thucydides in the Modern World* (Cambridge, 2012), and regular postings on http://thesphinxblog.com.
2 Karl Marx, 'Die achtzehnte Brumaire des Louis Bonaparte' [1851–2], in *Marx–Engels Werke* (Berlin, 1960), p. 116. My translation.
3 Christa Wolf, *Kassandra* (Darmstadt, 1983), pp. 133–4. My translation. Translated into English by Jan van Heurck as *Cassandra: a novel and four essays* (London, 1984).

Chapter 4 Anticipating the Future?

1 Thucydides 1.22.4.
2 Graham Allison, *Destined for War? Can America and China Escape Thucydides's Trap?* (New York, 2017). The Auden line comes from '1 September 1939' [1939], in *Another Time* (New York, 1940), p. 48.
3 Edward Gibbon, *The History of the Decline and Fall of the Roman Empire* [1776] (new edn, R. Priestley et al.: London, 1821). Quotes from Chapter 71, in Vol. 8, pp. 358–9; four causes of destruction on p. 362, elaborated over the following pages.

4 Constantin-François Volney, *Volney's Ruins: or, meditation on the revolutions of empires* [1794], trans. Thomas Jefferson & Joel Barlow (Paris, 1802), p. 15.

5 David Engels, *Le déclin: la crise de l'Union européenne et la chute de la République romaine* (Paris, 2012).

6 Morris Berman, *The Twilight of American Culture* (New York, 2000); 'Waiting for the Barbarians', *Guardian*, 5 October 2001 (https://www.theguardian.com/books/2001/oct/06/books.guardianreview5).

7 Friedrich Nietzsche, 'Vom Nutzen und Nachtheil der Historie für das Leben', *Unzeitgemässe Betrachtungen* [1874], in *Sämtliche Werke: Kritischen Studienausgabe* I, ed. G. Colli & M. Montinari (Berlin, 1967), p. 247. My translation.

Further Reading

General

Mary Beard & John Henderson, *Classics: a very short introduction* (Oxford, 1995)

Edith Hall, 'Classics for the People', *Guardian*, 20 June 2015: https://www.theguardian.com/books/2015/jun/20/classics-for-the-people-ancient-greeks

Dan-el Padilla Peralta, 'Why "Why Classics?"', Stanford University, Department of Classics: https://classics.stanford.edu/dan-el-padilla-peralta-why-why-classics

Josephine Crawley Quinn, 'Against Classics', Women's Classical Committee, 27 October 2017: https://wcc-uk.blogs.sas.ac.uk/2017/10/27/against-classics/

The online journal *Eidolon* (https://eidolon.pub/) is a reliable source of fascinating reflections on the study of the classics, especially in its relation to the modern world.

Further Reading

Chapter 1

Edith Hall, 'Putting the Class into Classical Reception', Royal Holloway, University of London: https://www.royalholloway.ac.uk/crgr/documents/pdf/papers/classicsandclass.pdf

Neville Morley, *Antiquity and Modernity* (Malden, MA, 2009)

Christopher Stray, *Classics Transformed: schools, universities, and society in England, 1830–1960* (Oxford, 1998)

Chapter 2

Useful introductions to the different sorts of evidence used in classical studies and ancient history can be found in two important series of books, *Approaching the Ancient World* (https://www.routledge.com/Approaching-the-Ancient-World/book-series/SE0153) from Routledge and *Key Themes in Ancient History* from Cambridge University Press (https://www.cambridge.org/core/series/key-themes-in-ancient-history/3DC870F8689FE12C7A855D858D93B9A0).

Chapter 3

Lorna Hardwick & Christopher Stray, eds, *A Companion to Classical Receptions* (Malden, MA, 2007)

Charles Martindale & Richard F. Thomas, eds, *Classics and the Uses of Reception* (Malden, MA, 2006)

Further Reading

Chapter 4

Peter Frase, *Four Futures: life after capitalism* (London, 2016)

Jo Walton, *The Just City* (New York, 2015); *The Philosopher Kings* (New York, 2015); and *Necessity* (New York, 2016)

Index

141

Index

Index